OPPOSING
VIEWPOINTS®
SERIES

The Impact of the Tech Giants

Other Books of Related Interest:

Opposing Viewpoints Series

Domestic Terrorism

Internet Censorship

Privacy

Robotic Technology

At Issue Series

Bitcoin

Does the Internet Increase Anxiety?

What Are the Jobs of the Future?

What Is the Impact of Twitter?

Current Controversies Series

Cybercrime

Drones

E-books

The Global Impact of Social Media

"Congress shall make no law . . . abridging the freedom of speech, or of the press."

First Amendment to the US Constitution

The basic foundation of our democracy is the First Amendment guarantee of freedom of expression. The Opposing Viewpoints series is dedicated to the concept of this basic freedom and the idea that it is more important to practice it than to enshrine it.

OPPOSING VIEWPOINTS® SERIES

The Impact of the Tech Giants

Jack Lasky, Book Editor

GREENHAVEN PRESS
A part of Gale, Cengage Learning

GALE
CENGAGE Learning·

Farmington Hills, Mich • San Francisco • New York • Waterville, Maine
Meriden, Conn • Mason, Ohio • Chicago

Judy Galens, *Manager, Frontlist Acquisitions*

For more information, contact:
Greenhaven Press
27500 Drake Rd.
Farmington Hills, MI 48331-3535
Or you can visit our Internet site at gale.cengage.com

For product information and technology assistance, contact us at

Gale Customer Support, 1-800-877-4253
For permission to use material from this text or product, submit all requests online at www.cengage.com/permissions

Further permissions questions can be emailed to permissionrequest@cengage.com

LIBRARY OF CONGRESS CATALOGING-IN-PUBLICATION DATA

The impact of the tech giants / Jack Lasky, book editor.
    pages cm. -- (Opposing viewpoints)
  Includes bibliographical references and index.
  ISBN 978-0-7377-7522-8 (hardcover) -- ISBN 978-0-7377-7523-5 (pbk.)
  1. Technology--Social aspects. 2. High technology industries--United States.
  3. Social responsibility of business. I. Lasky, Jack, editor.
  T14.5.I47 2016
  338.4'760973--dc23
                            2015029840

Printed in the United States of America
1 2 3 4 5   20 19 18 17 16

Contents

Chapter 3: What Are Some Common Criticisms of Tech Giants?

Chapter 4: What Does the Future Hold for Tech Giants?

Why Consider Opposing Viewpoints?

> *"The only way in which a human being can make some approach to knowing the whole of a subject is by hearing what can be said about it by persons of every variety of opinion and studying all modes in which it can be looked at by every character of mind. No wise man ever acquired his wisdom in any mode but this."*
>
> *John Stuart Mill*

In our media-intensive culture it is not difficult to find differing opinions. Thousands of newspapers and magazines and dozens of radio and television talk shows resound with differing points of view. The difficulty lies in deciding which opinion to agree with and which "experts" seem the most credible. The more inundated we become with differing opinions and claims, the more essential it is to hone critical reading and thinking skills to evaluate these ideas. Opposing Viewpoints books address this problem directly by presenting stimulating debates that can be used to enhance and teach these skills. The varied opinions contained in each book examine many different aspects of a single issue. While examining these conveniently edited opposing views, readers can develop critical thinking skills such as the ability to compare and contrast authors' credibility, facts, argumentation styles, use of persuasive techniques, and other stylistic tools. In short, the Opposing Viewpoints Series is an ideal way to attain the higher-level thinking and reading skills so essential in a culture of diverse and contradictory opinions.

In addition to providing a tool for critical thinking, Opposing Viewpoints books challenge readers to question their own strongly held opinions and assumptions. Most people form their opinions on the basis of upbringing, peer pressure, and personal, cultural, or professional bias. By reading carefully balanced opposing views, readers must directly confront new ideas as well as the opinions of those with whom they disagree. This is not to argue simplistically that everyone who reads opposing views will—or should—change his or her opinion. Instead, the series enhances readers' understanding of their own views by encouraging confrontation with opposing ideas. Careful examination of others' views can lead to the readers' understanding of the logical inconsistencies in their own opinions, perspective on why they hold an opinion, and the consideration of the possibility that their opinion requires further evaluation.

Evaluating Other Opinions

To ensure that this type of examination occurs, Opposing Viewpoints books present all types of opinions. Prominent spokespeople on different sides of each issue as well as well-known professionals from many disciplines challenge the reader. An additional goal of the series is to provide a forum for other, less known, or even unpopular viewpoints. The opinion of an ordinary person who has had to make the decision to cut off life support from a terminally ill relative, for example, may be just as valuable and provide just as much insight as a medical ethicist's professional opinion. The editors have two additional purposes in including these less known views. One, the editors encourage readers to respect others' opinions—even when not enhanced by professional credibility. It is only by reading or listening to and objectively evaluating others' ideas that one can determine whether they are worthy of consideration. Two, the inclusion of such viewpoints encourages the important critical thinking skill of objectively evaluating an author's credentials and bias. This evaluation will illuminate an author's reasons for taking a particular stance on an issue and will aid in readers' evaluation of the author's ideas.

It is our hope that these books will give readers a deeper understanding of the issues debated and an appreciation of the complexity of even seemingly simple issues when good and honest people disagree. This awareness is particularly important in a democratic society such as ours in which people enter into public debate to determine the common good. Those with whom one disagrees should not be regarded as enemies but rather as people whose views deserve careful examination and may shed light on one's own.

Thomas Jefferson once said that "difference of opinion leads to inquiry, and inquiry to truth." Jefferson, a broadly educated man, argued that "if a nation expects to be ignorant and free . . . it expects what never was and never will be." As individuals and as a nation, it is imperative that we consider the opinions of others and examine them with skill and discernment. The Opposing Viewpoints series is intended to help readers achieve this goal.

David L. Bender and Bruno Leone,
Founders

Introduction

"The iconic view of tech companies almost invariably [stresses] their roots in people's garages, plucky individual entrepreneurs ready to challenge all comers. Yet increasingly the leading tech firms . . . have morphed into vast tech conglomerates, with hands in ever more numerous, and sometimes not obvious, fields of endeavor."

—*Joel Kotkin,*
"How a Few Monster Tech Firms
Are Taking Over Everything from
Media to Space Travel and What
It Means for the Rest of Us,"
The Daily Beast, February 9, 2014

For decades, computer and technology companies have been the largest and most successful businesses in America and around the world. Tech giants such as Facebook, Apple, Google, and Amazon have become some of the most recognizable brand names in existence and have established themselves as the world's undisputed leaders in technological innovation. As a result of their immense size and extensive reach, these tech giants also have come to hold a great deal of influence over the way we live our lives and the direction in which we are moving as a society. Given the extent of this influence, it can hardly be surprising that the impact of the tech giants is great.

The story of how the tech giants have become such a major part of the modern world began with the rise of Silicon Valley, a region of Southern California famous for being the heart of the tech industry. Although the Silicon Valley nickname was not coined until 1971, the region has been associated with technology since the 1950s. The transformation of the region, which was previously a noted agricultural hub, began when Stanford University founded a research park there in 1951. Stanford's research park was designed to be a location where the school and private companies could conduct technological research together. Later in the decade, as companies such as Shockley Semiconductor Laboratory and Fairchild Semiconductor were established in the future Silicon Valley, the region gained widespread recognition as America's capital of technological innovation.

By the time Silicon Valley took on its familiar name in the 1970s, many of the companies based there had shifted from primarily depending on military contracts to focusing on the growing commercial computer market. Over the next two decades, Silicon Valley became increasingly identified with the computer industry and the manufacture of microchips. It was during this period that some of the valley's biggest and most successful resident companies, including Microsoft and Apple, were first founded. After losing some ground to Japanese tech companies in the 1980s, Silicon Valley rebounded in the 1990s, particularly with the emergence of the Internet and e-commerce, around 1995. By the end of the decade, the valley was home to a whole new cadre of Internet-based tech companies including Google and Yahoo. Although not all of these companies survived in the long term, many of those that did gradually evolved into sprawling corporate empires as technologies such as computers, cell phones, and tablets became increasingly ubiquitous.

Today's tech giants are bigger and more powerful than any of their earlier predecessors and even most other contemporary corporations. While many of these companies still call Silicon Valley home, some of the largest are actively branching out to cities around the country and the world in a bid to increase their reach and influence even further. As might be expected, the meteoric rise of these tech behemoths—especially titans such as Apple, Google, Amazon, and Microsoft—has not been without controversy or criticism. Detractors have long questioned the true intentions of these companies and whether they pose a threat to the free market or even society in general. Concerns often have been raised about the business practices in which these entities engage, the quality and worth of the products they produce and sell, the way tech giants affect our lives, and the way their business practices impact the environment and the world around us.

Opposing Viewpoints: The Impact of the Tech Giants examines the role technology companies play in today's world in chapters titled "How Do Tech Giants Impact Society?," "What Issues Surround the Products of Tech Giants?," "What Are Some Common Criticisms of Tech Giants?," and "What Does the Future Hold for Tech Giants?" Undoubtedly, the rise and continued dominance of technology companies has been a controversial and much debated topic. This volume offers insight into this debate from an array of different perspectives.

CHAPTER 1

How Do Tech Giants Impact Society?

Chapter Preface

A s technology has become a bigger part of everyday life over the years, tech giants such as Facebook, Apple, Google, and Microsoft have, in many ways, irrevocably changed the American social landscape. Whether that change has been for better or worse, however, is a matter of some debate. Generally speaking, big technology companies tend to present themselves as more socially progressive and forward thinking than most big businesses. While that might be true at least to some extent, critics argue that they are just as profit driven and corrupt as other corporate entities. With all that said, what impact have tech giants really had on society?

In practice, there are numerous ways to judge the impact tech giants have had on society. The most obvious and straightforward way is to simply look at how socially responsible big tech companies are. While some see tech giants as far more socially responsible than other corporations, others contend that these companies often adhere to policies and practices that only serve to broaden social divides. Another way to judge the social responsibility of tech giants is to look at the way they respond to major social issues. For example, some experts believe that big tech companies are taking a stand in the fight against National Security Agency (NSA) surveillance. On the other hand, critics say that such companies have actually been complicit in the NSA's efforts to spy on civilians. Similarly, one can also gauge tech giants' social responsibility by looking at how proactive they are about environmental issues. Although it could be argued that many tech companies put more effort into being environmentally friendly than other companies, some critics believe that they still are not doing enough.

One way to determine just how socially responsible tech giants are is to look at the effect they are having on urban communities. As tech giants establish an increasing number of headquarters, data centers, and other facilities in cities such as San Francisco and Pittsburgh, the neighborhoods they are moving into are undergoing a swift transformation. In some communities, such as Pittsburgh's Larimer neighborhood, the arrival of tech giants is seen as a beneficial development that is boosting the local economy, improving living conditions, and generally making the area a better place to live. In places like San Francisco's Mission District, however, the growing influx of tech workers is viewed as detrimental by locals who feel like they are being pushed out of their neighborhoods by a wave of tech gentrification, wherein affluent tech employees are moving in and displacing poorer residents. Whether the effect is negative or positive, it is clear that the impact of the tech giants is being felt in a big way in America's cities.

Given their size and the degree to which their products have become an indispensable part of modern life, tech giants find themselves in a position to influence the development of today's society. The decisions they make and the way they do business have an enormous social impact. As a result, it is critical that they remain socially conscious and aware of all the implications their actions have.

The following chapter examines how tech companies affect society. The topics explored include the social responsibility of tech giants, tech giants' view of government surveillance, and the impact tech giants and their products have on the environment, local communities, and the world.

> "It's becoming more clear that innovation by the multibillion-dollar companies who power our increasingly precious resource called the Internet, and the passion behind environmentalism, don't have to be mutually exclusive."

Tech Giants Are Socially Responsible

Lyndsey Gilpin

In the following viewpoint, Lyndsey Gilpin argues that tech giants are demonstrating their social consciousness by actively making environmentally responsible decisions. Specifically, she cites the fact that many big tech companies are making a concerted effort to use only renewable sources of energy as evidence that the tech industry is seriously invested in social issues. Gilpin is a staff writer for TechRepublic *who focuses on tech leadership, sustainability, and social entrepreneurship.*

As you read, consider the following questions:

1. According to Gilpin, what kind of energy is primarily powering the Internet and much of the tech industry at present?

2. According to Gilpin, why are tech companies now in a position to impact environmental change?

3. According to Gilpin, how have tech companies empowered individuals in the struggle for environmental reform?

Loudoun County, Virginia, is home to more than 4.3 million square feet of data centers and claims that 70% of Internet traffic flows through it every single day. It hosts the servers of many major tech companies, and because of that, it has enormous influence on the world—even though hardly anyone knows its name.

But the county—its data centers, its people, its economy, its land—is still in the hands of the coal industry.

Clean energy has shown renewed signs of progress in 2014, and it has energized environmentalists, technologists, social entrepreneurs, and educators alike. This year [2014], the tech industry in particular has received a lot of praise for its work toward renewable energy.

Photos of solar panels on the roofs of giant corporate buildings, vast wind farms sprawling across the desert, and massive hydropower plants along the coasts are widely circulated. Start-ups in Silicon Valley and around the world have focused efforts on solving problems facing the energy sector such as battery storage, energy transmission, and big data analytics. Companies have become more transparent about their environmental practices and scaled up their efforts in corporate social responsibility.

But the truth of the matter is, large-scale improvement—like significant reduction in greenhouse gas emissions and the slowing of climate change—doesn't happen when tech companies narrowly focus on their own operations and build their facilities in already environmentally progressive states like California or Nevada.

It happens when they get involved with states like Virginia.

How Big Tech Is Powered

Dominion Energy [Solutions] is the utility provider for Virginia, and coal and natural gas accounted for 98% of its electricity in 2013. Only 2% was from renewables. The state of Virginia is a leading coal producer; about 4.5% of US coal production east of the Mississippi River in 2012 came from the state. And Norfolk, Virginia, America's largest coal export facility, processed more than 38% of US coal exports that year, according to the Energy Information Administration [EIA].

So if it's true that the majority of Internet traffic flows through the servers in Loudoun County, and the majority of tech companies still rely on coal, that means that the majority of the Internet continues to be powered by finite fossil fuels.

According to Greenpeace's most recent report, the cloud consumes as much energy as what would be the world's sixth largest country. After Greenpeace began calling out the world's largest tech companies a few years ago, Apple, Google, Facebook, and others vowed to power their data centers with 100% renewable energy. Apple and Facebook have built new data centers that run on 100% renewable energy, and Google is more than a third of the way to that goal.

But Amazon, the other tech giant, remained silent until several weeks ago. The company finally announced in a low-key statement on its website that Amazon Web Services (AWS)—its cloud computing division—has a "long-term commitment to achieve 100% renewable energy usage for our global infrastructure footprint."

AWS servers host Netflix, Pinterest, Spotify, Vine, Airbnb, and many other websites. According to David Pomerantz, media officer for Greenpeace, Amazon operates at least 10 data centers in its "US-East" region, and its largest is in northern Virginia.

"We don't know exactly how much electricity Amazon uses there, since the company still hasn't published that data, but it's safe to say that it's a lot. We and other analysts have estimated that over half of Amazon's servers are in this region," he said.

Making the Transition

The transition to renewable energy will affect many people, because fossil fuels are embedded deeply in Virginia's culture and economy. But it's an issue that will eventually surface in every state as the US and the world move forward to tackle energy sustainability and climate change.

Economic effects, difficulty of implementation, and fear of the unknown are just some of the reasons lawmakers stalemate over environmental policy changes and why they become so politicized. But now, tech companies are starting to fill the gaps that the government won't, while serving as examples of how relatively fast and cost-effective it is to make these changes.

Where governments lack speed, the tech industry moves at a staggering pace. Utilities lack efficiency; technology companies are obsessed with innovation. Many of these communities lack funding or people to affect change; tech giants have both. And where environmental organizations cause polarizing debates, tech companies remain mostly neutral.

Amazon has a choice to move forward with its pledge— and it will involve, as most progress does—getting entangled with state and federal laws, the utility industry, fossil fuel companies, and various stakeholders.

Of course, the company's decision in Loudoun County is only one example in this larger picture of progress. But it's an important one. Amazon, who declined to comment on its commitment to use renewable energy in its data centers, is now at a very public crossroads.

Because it has such a footprint on the East Coast, where coal reigns king, it has a chance to make a difference in the way Loudoun County is powered—and maybe, how renewable energy is addressed in the future.

"Amazon could do any number of things, including pushing Dominion to improve that offering, pushing them to invest in more renewable energy, buying renewable energy from another provider, or pushing state policy makers to tear down some of the barriers to renewable energy growth in Virginia," said Pomerantz. "What it really can't do, if it wants to make good on its new 100% renewable energy pledge, is sit still."

State of Affairs

In 2013, renewable energy accounted for about 10% of total US energy consumption and 13% of electricity generation, according to the EIA. And at the state level, there isn't much preparation either. A study earlier this year from Georgetown Climate Center showed that less than half of US states are preparing for the looming effects of climate change.

This year, President [Barack] Obama finally addressed climate change by instituting the first ever federal ruling, the Clean Power Plan, to cut carbon emissions by 30% under 2005 levels by 2030. But recently, the EPA [Environmental Protection Agency] has discussed an extension for the ruling after much lobbying by utility companies during the past few months.

Greenhouse gas emissions increased at their fastest rate in 30 years in 2013, according to the World Meteorological Organization. The National Oceanic and Atmospheric Administration (NOAA) reported that January to October of 2014 had the highest global temperatures on record.

A Global Conversation

Addressing climate change is a global conversation, and with the rapid growth of technology around the world, it is becoming even more urgent, public, and connected.

According to the US census, almost 75% of the US population has access to the Internet. Over half of American adults use their cell phone to go online, according to Pew Research [Center].

China is expected to have 200 million new Internet users by 2015, and companies such as Amazon are planning to open China-based data centers to meet that demand. In 2011, between 1.5% and 3% of energy generation in China went toward powering the Internet. And although people in emerging markets are largely off-line, the Internet, particularly on smartphones, has seen tremendous growth, and people who get it integrate it into their lives very quickly.

The tech industry is starting to use that power, money, and growth to affect positive change in areas where government efforts are stagnant. That's not necessarily driven by altruism, of course—it's just good business. But since the tech industry is driven by competitiveness, these clean energy moves are becoming effective in building a movement.

"In addition to the environmental benefits, we see renewable energy as a business opportunity," said a Google spokesperson. "Perhaps most importantly, we look for scalable solutions that can have the highest possible impact. It's great if we solve a problem for ourselves, but we also want to be looking for opportunities to directly address problems that limit the growth of renewable energy. Over the years we've been open and shared our approach to renewable energy with the industry (and the public) in a series of white papers, blog posts and events."

Google is also drawing a few lines in the sand. In 2014, the company withdrew from the American Legislative Exchange Council (ALEC) and executive chairman Eric Schmidt said ALEC was "just literally lying" when denying climate change. Microsoft withdrew its support from ALEC back in 2012.

The Move to Clean Energy

However, it's not only the tech behemoths who are standing up for the environment. Salesforce, Box, and Rackspace are also leading the way in environmental responsibility, committing to 100% renewable energy, setting attainable goals each year to reach that point, and making sure they're transparent about it.

"I do think that has a huge effect," Pomerantz said. "It's a big effect on the business community, a lot of people who maybe don't care what Greenpeace has to think about climate change, they're more impressed [with that]."

This momentum throughout the industry—and particularly, the leadership shown by big tech companies—has potential, said Matthew Stepp, executive director of the Center for Clean Energy [Innovation]. And the action from those companies shows that it just makes economic sense.

"It's absolutely true that the economic influence of companies like Amazon will push some of these states to act more flexibly when it comes to their energy mix because it's easy for Amazon to move elsewhere that is more amenable to its sustainability demands," Stepp said.

Ultimately, he said, he believes states will make it work because it means more jobs within their borders. Whether that flips a state to adopt very aggressive clean energy policies remains to be seen, though. Many of the states will probably be able to accommodate renewable energy practices without implementing really aggressive policies like carbon pricing or portfolio standards.

He added: "I think that goes to show that economic influence will be a bigger driver of expanding clean energy than just environmental well-being."

The Long-Standing Movement

Technology and nature have been at odds throughout history. But tech companies now have the knowledge and resources to affect change—so they now have a choice. They are no longer dependent on one source of energy, and most of the time, they aren't dependent on the government.

"Flexible policy is critical as well as continued support for technology development that opens up new opportunities for these companies to offer more innovative, efficient technologies, as well as reduce their carbon footprint even more," Stepp said.

The environmental movement has been viewed as a left-wing liberal push since the radical events of the 1960s. The iconic image for most people is probably of a dirty protester chained to a tree, or lying in front of a bulldozer. It's the movement that spawned Greenpeace, PETA [People for the Ethical Treatment of Animals], NRDC [Natural Resources Defense Council]. It's the movement that called dramatic attention to climate change and global warming that made them seem like they were optional to believe. But it has successfully served the public good by advocating for cleaner water, expansion of protected lands for parks and forests, safer working environments for coal miners, preservation of biodiversity, and more.

Awareness around the need for an environmental movement started in the 19th century, after the Industrial Revolution, when coal burned at an unprecedented rate in major cities because of vast, rapid growth and innovation, and pollution from factories poured into the air, and chemical waste flowed into water sources. The first environmental law—the Alkali Act—was passed in 1863 in Britain to regulate pollution.

Early on, radical environmental ideals were pushed by individuals and organizations. They banded together to stop coal pollution, to conserve natural lands, to safely sanitize cities. In the late 19th century, literature on the subject by Henry David Thoreau, and the establishment of the Sierra Club by John Muir, ignited the movement.

It wasn't until the 1950s that the movement truly started to take off in the US. As technological innovation progressed, people began to realize it often came at a cost to the natural world. So began the backlash against chemical companies. The Nature Conservancy was established in 1951. The Air Pollution Control Act was passed in 1955. Carbon dioxide levels raised to 300 parts per million during the decade, and NGOs [nongovernmental organizations] like the Sierra Club started to gain recognition for their protests.

Then, in 1962, it got much more serious. Rachel Carson published *Silent Spring*, and it became the catalyst for the modern environmental movement. Largely because of her work, DDT [dichlorodiphenyltrichloroethane]—which had been considered a miracle of modern technology—was banned in 1972. Perhaps the most important aspect of Carson's book, though, was her warning against technological innovation— that humans should not ruin nature with their progress. But she didn't call for federal regulations, because the government could be in the hands of the industries that were destroying the planet. She wanted the people to understand those processes and their consequences.

Fast-forward to today: The current grid system is about to be turned upside down, because of renewable energy technologies. People, companies, and communities now have the opportunity to generate their own power by installing solar panels, and they don't want utility companies to make all of the money off of it.

Technological innovation—and by default, tech companies—have a big role to play in this conversation, because no one has quite figured out the formula yet.

"New business models will be at the heart of transforming [and] accelerating adoption of renewable energy at scale. Right now we have a lot of big renewable deals where one large entity creates their own private energy, or deals that only work when there are incentives," said Melissa Gray, senior director of corporate social responsibility for Rackspace. "Not everyone can do that, so we need more options for different sized players and that make sense long term to scale out."

The Risk of Too Much Talk

Earlier this year, Pew Research [Center] asked participants of a study if they thought "environmentalist" described them. More than 40% of respondents agreed—with the exception of millennials. Only 32% of them said yes. NPR looked into the phenomenon and found that millennials (18 to 33 year olds) felt like the term has been corrupted or too politicized. Many of them want to be known for doing good for the environment, and supporting those causes—but they're not committed to the label.

However, one thing millennials—and really, most people in general—are fairly committed to is their favorite technology companies. The people who will wait in line for three days at the Apple Store will probably also back Tim Cook's bold stance on the environment.

Getting involved with the government is important, Gray said, but rallying fans can be just as critical. And that has proven true. Tech companies, though they may be scolded for their fickle privacy policies, pointless software updates, and expensive tools, are generally well trusted by the public to be progressive and do good for the world.

"Rackspace opted to define an energy policy to rally 'Rackers' around how we thought about it and our resultant actions," Gray added. "We continue to work internally to define our advocacy strategy. We'll be doing more in 2015 in these areas."

Big Tech, Watchdogs and Transparency

Environmental organizations like Greenpeace have always been watchdogs for the environment. Now, though, as the world continually becomes more connected, and people have the ability to track their products and their personal impact on the world, everyone has the power to monitor and pressure companies to clean up their acts.

But looking into these things isn't necessarily associating with environmentalism. It's simply understanding the way businesses work. Companies want to be able to tell stories about doing good to strengthen their brands and build stronger bonds with customers. It's why each year, new companies take Greenpeace's pledge.

It's why transparency is lauded more than ever. And it's why companies are widely promoting their corporate social responsibility work. Some are even going a step further and becoming benefit corporations.

The danger with all of this is greenwashing. As people focus more on the future of the planet, companies realize they can fare better in the public eye with these commitments, and make them without a real plan of action.

"Amazon's 100% commitment, we were certainly excited to see," Pomerantz said. "But a wave of happy stories without any action . . . we have to make sure that is a conversation."

Another big risk is that companies like Amazon start to clean up their own power sources because of the pressure from customers and the industry, but they only do so myopically.

"For the tech sector to really leverage all of its influence, it needs to impact government decisions as well," Pomerantz said. "The risk is . . . they focus just on those in the narrowest sense without trying to change the broader system around them."

Making a Difference

Working on their own processes is key for morale and branding, but as for impacting climate change, it doesn't make much of a difference. Rather, Stepp said, tech companies are mostly influencing consumer behavior through their products, like Google buying Nest [Labs], AT&T and its work on connected cars, Verizon and its smart home technologies.

This extends to start-ups in the industry, as well. As the clean-tech space becomes more crowded, it's important to make sure companies are moving the narrative in the right direction: awareness, then action—which could be the key to influence other industries such as energy, retail, travel, and manufacturing.

If they don't, they're leaving a lot of opportunity unfulfilled. For them as successful businesses. For recruiting potential customers. For garnering good press. And for preserving the environment.

"The tech companies won't usher in the grand low-carbon energy transformation we need, but they will be an enabler of it," Stepp said.

The Next Wave

2015 will be a telling one for clean technology. Not only will climate change politics come to be more defined and regulations brought to the table, but technologies will have to expand beyond California to areas—like Virginia—that are more reluctant to adopt them.

Apple made a realistic energy goal and achieved it. From the moment the company pledged it would power data centers with renewable energy, it only took two years for them to go from fossil fuels to 100% clean energy. To make those changes, Apple had to work with Duke Energy, the largest utility in the US, which uses mostly coal and nuclear plants to power its grid.

The combined lobbying of Apple, Google, and Facebook, who all have data center projects in North Carolina, has forced Duke to make even larger scale changes since then. The utility announced it will build three solar facilities in the state and it has also signed five power purchase agreements (PPAs) with solar energy generation developers, which means $500 million invested in renewable energy and 278 megawatts of generated solar power for the state. That's just a piece of its broader plan to invest $2 billion in renewable power around the world by 2018.

With PPAs, which are long-term financial commitments to buy renewable energy through specific utilities, tech companies have dramatically impacted the way states develop clean energy facilities. For example, Google has five large-scale PPAs in places like Iowa, Oklahoma, and Sweden. They've also worked with Duke in North Carolina to create a green tariff that allows them and other large energy customers to more easily choose renewable energy. As Google and other companies rapidly grow their footprints in states like Oregon, Utah, and Iowa, they have brought with them changes to utility agreements and energy policies.

But while tech companies lobby utilities, the fossil fuel industry is lobbying lawmakers to make it more difficult for people to buy or lease renewable energy and curb environmental rules.

"We would like to see the industry come together to reach a point where choosing renewable energy is easy, where regulatory and market barriers are minimized and anyone who wants renewable energy has access to it," said a Google spokesperson.

The energy and tech industries will have to work together to make net metering (the way utilities resell renewable energy generated by homes) and permitting—which are both processes that often make installing solar more expensive and slow—easier.

Consumers and businesses will also have to put pressure on the utility industry so that they can fully benefit from the energy they generate from their own renewable energy sources such as solar.

An Opportunity for Change

Climate change and sustainability are global issues, and tech companies can't deal with them without reaching beyond the boundaries of their own facilities and operations. That will require more talks with policy makers, more lobbying, and more fights with the fossil fuel industry, which has a huge stake and influence in government operations around the world.

Sitting in a boardroom in talks with Dominion Energy executives isn't as photogenic as a beautiful sprawling wind farm in Texas, but it does present an important opportunity for these companies to rework the narrative of climate change policy.

"Companies can think big and aim not to sort of clean up their problem in the narrowest way possible, but to really create [systemic] change," Pomerantz said.

Many years of stereotypes, radical protests and campaigns, and lawsuits have plagued the environmental movement. But the world is moving from paper to digital; from large-scale manufacturing to custom creation; and from coal plants to solar farms. It's becoming more clear that innovation by the multibillion-dollar companies who power our increasingly precious resource called the Internet, and the passion behind environmentalism, don't have to be mutually exclusive. And they certainly don't have to be enemies.

In fact, the combination of the two might be humanity's best hope to drive swift and significant changes in the years ahead.

> *"A 2015 report . . . found that three in ten Silicon Valley residents don't earn enough to support themselves; this includes many of tech's invisible workers—the security officers, shuttle drivers, janitors, cooks and landscapers—who are supporting an industry that is pricing them out."*

The New Silicon Valley Movement That Is Taking On the Tech Giants

Gabriel Thompson

In the following viewpoint, Gabriel Thompson argues that tech giants in Silicon Valley are demonstrating social irresponsibility by underpaying their service workers. He contends that the tech industry's business practices are stymying the economic mobility of low-wage workers and keeping them trapped in a never-ending culture of poverty. He adds that despite the fact that some tech companies have taken steps to combat this problem, it remains a major issue that needs to be addressed immediately.

Thompson is an author whose published works include Working in the Shadows: A Year of Doing the Jobs (Most) Americans Won't Do *and* America's Social Arsonist: Fred Ross and Grassroots Organizing in the Twentieth Century.

As you read, consider the following questions:

1. According to Thompson, what have Google and Apple done to make working conditions fairer for their security workers?

2. According to Thompson, why is it unlikely that the economy alone will improve Silicon Valley's poverty problem?

3. According to Thompson, how has the Affordable Housing Network helped the problem of poverty in Silicon Valley?

On a warm afternoon in late February [2015], 200 people filed into the social hall of Our Lady of Guadalupe Parish, set back from a busy street on San Jose's eastside. The large crowd was excited and boisterous—the event has been months in the making—with people calling out loud greetings to each other in Spanish and English. During a quiet moment, Chava Bustamante stepped up to the podium. A longtime union organizer, he now runs a group called LUNA—Latinos United for a New America—whose logo was emblazoned across his bright yellow shirt. "Make a mental note of today," he told the group. "When we look back, we're going to say, 'I was part of this historic moment.'"

The moment he was referring to was the launch of Silicon Valley Rising. Born in the heart of a booming tech empire, this broad coalition of labor, community and faith groups hopes to use that boom to benefit, instead of displace, the working poor. Apple's headquarters in Cupertino is just a dozen miles away. Facebook is farther down the highway, in Menlo Park. But those tech companies are only one side of the valley, with their sleek gadgets and social networks and, above all, enormous wealth. This modest social hall, with its cracked ceiling tiles and twice-a-week food service to the hungry, was a reminder that out here, in the center of all that is new and shiny, the age-old problem of poverty persists.

A group of young Latinas stepped forward to share their vision for the future: a Silicon Valley where tents are only used for camping, not as shelters of last resort; where workers are no longer invisible and disposable; where paychecks cover the cost of housing and food. These dreams sound basic, but they are ambitious. Rents in San Jose increased 13 percent last year [2014], to a median that now exceeds $3,000 a month. Until recently the city was home to "the Jungle," reported to be the largest homeless encampment in the nation. A 2015 report from the Silicon Valley Institute for Regional Studies found that three in ten Silicon Valley residents don't earn enough to support themselves; this includes many of tech's invisible workers—the security officers, shuttle drivers, janitors, cooks and landscapers—who are supporting an industry that is pricing them out.

"Things are definitely getting worse," said Michael Johnson, during an interview several days later. Johnson is an officer with Universal Protection Service, a large security contractor that the union seeks to organize. He has spent a decade guarding tech offices for a handful of security companies, and has seen his pay remain flat—as he puts it, "not a whole lot more than the minimum wage"—and benefits disappear. He lives in a rented room, depending on donated food from a friend, a fellow guard whose work site has catered meals. He places the blame squarely on the high-tech companies, who have forced contractors to cut costs to win bids.

"We've participated in their success," he said of the tech industry. "Why can't we participate in their prosperity?"

Poverty in Silicon Valley

Can the outsized influence of tech somehow be harnessed to benefit low-wage workers in Silicon Valley?

While this is still a distant dream, there are some promising signs. When anti-gentrification protesters stood in front of Google buses last winter, the news traveled far and wide. Less well known is that the drivers who shuttle tech workers to and fro are going union. Last fall, the drivers at Loop Transportation who drive for Facebook voted to join the Teamsters [International Brotherhood of Teamsters]. Before, their wages averaged $17.93 an hour, and some paid $1,200 a month for family health insurance. Under their new contract, wages increased by an average of $5.73 an hour and health care is entirely covered by the employer.

Meanwhile, at the end of February, the Teamsters celebrated another victory, when workers at Compass Transportation, which shuttles employees at Apple, eBay, Genentech, Yahoo and Zynga, voted 104–38 to join the union. "It's on the fringe of even being able to support a family, still," admits Rome Aloise, a Teamsters vice president, about the new contracts. "Frankly, what it means to these companies is about what they spend on ping-pong balls for the year." Still, it is a start, and the Teamsters, who are members of Silicon Valley Rising, hope that their success will embolden other contracted workers on tech campuses to organize.

There is also evidence that the tech companies can be moved. Last fall, after a lengthy campaign by SEIU [Service Employees International Union], Google got rid of Security Industry Specialists (SIS), and took the security workers in house, where they receive the same generous benefits as other Google employees. And on March 3, Apple, which Silicon Valley Rising had planned to protest at its shareholder meeting today, announced that it was following Google's lead and ditching SIS as well. Guards will now be Apple employees, receiving paid family health care and retirement benefits (and presumably, raises).

These one-off fights targeting the world's most recognizable companies have highlighted the plight of tech's impoverished service workers, but the coalition plans to scale up quickly. "We have to convince the private sector to change strategies," says Derecka Mehrens, the executive director of Working Partnerships USA, a community-labor alliance that was critical to the formation of Silicon Valley Rising. "They are driving major income inequality—but we can show them there is a model" to help combat this inequality.

The model is based on the innovative living wage ordinance advocates pushed through Santa Clara County last fall, which covers the 17,000 employees whose companies do business with the county. Along with a minimum wage of $19.06 an hour, the measure provides workers with protection against unpredictable scheduling and anti-union harassment. The challenge now is to get the tech industry to voluntarily agree to similar standards.

A Serious Problem

Left unchecked, the economy—no matter how fast it grows—will do little to raise people out of poverty. There are 1.1 million low-wage workers in the Bay Area, which includes Silicon Valley, and it is projected that only about 310,000 middle-class jobs will be created by 2020. Members of the coalition have played a key role in trying to raise the floor for these low-wage workers. In 2012, they spearheaded San Jose's successful ballot measure to increase the minimum wage to $10 an hour, an improbable effort that grew out of the class project of a group of undergraduate students at San Jose State University. And other cities in Silicon Valley are following suit, including Sunnyvale and Mountain View—home to Google—which raised the minimum wage last fall to $10.30 with plans to increase it to $15 an hour. But coalition members see these efforts as only the beginning of a long project to turn traditionally low-wage jobs into something more sustainable.

"What we're talking about is occupational segregation," says Ben Field of the South Bay Labor Council. "We believe this problem cannot be solved without major reforms."

The other giant challenge is housing. Last fall, San Jose passed a new surcharge for developers, which the city expects to raise as much as $30 million a year to fund the construction of affordable housing. "The problem is that we need billions," says Mehrens of Working Partnerships. Much of the state funding has long since dried up, and the coalition hopes to bring tech on board to push for new solutions. While it will be a big lift to get tech to the table, Mehrens says that there is already a natural interest, as executives often cite the need to house their workforce as one of their most pressing concerns.

More immediately, coalition partners like the Affordable Housing Network seek to strengthen San Jose's weak rent protections, which allow landlords to raise rents 8 percent a year, and bar landlords from rejecting applicants simply because they receive Section 8 housing subsidies. (In California, such discrimination is legal.)

Robert Aguirre lived with his wife in the sprawling homeless encampment known as the Jungle until it was dismantled by the city last December. The 61-year-old was lucky enough to find a landlord that would accept his subsidy, but he knows many people who are still searching for a home. He now spends his days coordinating food deliveries and trash pickups at the dispersed homeless camps that have sprouted up in the wake of the Jungle's closure. "People out here are in survival mode," he said. "They are evicted from camp after camp, but there is nowhere for them to go. This can be a very hostile city."

A History of Poverty and Activism

Back in east San Jose, the people who had gathered at the church social hall knew all about the challenges facing the working poor. They also knew the road ahead would not be easy. But the mood was still upbeat and the event ended with optimistic chants of "*¡Sí se puede!*" [Yes, it is possible!] Many of the speakers likened their current fight to that of the late farmworker leader Cesar Chavez, who lived just a few blocks away from the church and whose turn to organizing was encouraged by a local activist priest named Father Donald Mc-Donnell, for whom the social hall where the group was gathered had been named.

That was back in the early 1950s, before the computer revolution, when this area was still known as the Santa Clara Valley. Much has changed since then, but there is still much that is recognizable. In Chavez's day, the region relied upon the invisible workers—mostly Latino—who spent long days in the surrounding fields and orchards, harvesting the bounty that helped make the state an agricultural powerhouse. Today it is still mostly people of color who do much of the valley's invisible labor, including those who put in long hours cleaning and protecting tech's sparkling campuses.

"It was here in this neighborhood that Cesar Chavez began his work," Ben Field of the South Bay Labor Council, told the crowd. "And it is here that we have chosen to begin our work—toward a new vision for Silicon Valley where all workers are valued."

> *"The corporate giants of technology are urging the US government to change its surveillance ways—and leading the way are the primary architects of the social networks now generating a distinctly modern mingling of commerce, selfies, and status updates."*

Why Tech Giants Are Now Uniting Against US Surveillance

Harry Bruinius

In the following viewpoint, Harry Bruinius argues that tech giants are a powerful force for change in relation to government surveillance because they have a vested interest in ensuring that consumers trust them. He asserts that big tech companies are leading the fight against excessive government surveillance because they realize how important it is for them to protect their users' data and demonstrate to users that they can be trusted with private information. Bruinius is an editor and a writer with the Christian Science Monitor.

As you read, consider the following questions:

1. According to Bruinius, what activity is the lifeblood of most big tech companies?

2. According to Bruinius, what is MUSCULAR, who runs it, and what does it do?

3. According to Aram Sinnreich, why is taking a stand against government surveillance particularly important for tech giants on an international scale?

The corporate giants of technology are urging the US government to change its surveillance ways—and leading the way are the primary architects of the social networks now generating a distinctly modern mingling of commerce, selfies, and status updates.

On Monday [December 9, 2013], a coalition of eight companies, including Facebook, Google, and Microsoft, sent an open letter to President [Barack] Obama and members of Congress, urging them to comply with "established global norms of free expression and privacy." It all but demanded the government work to ensure that all law enforcement and intelligence efforts "are rule-bound, narrowly tailored, transparent, and subject to oversight."

The missive suggests that these companies, which were joined by LinkedIn, Twitter, and Yahoo, have perceived government surveillance worldwide as a looming threat to the lifeblood of their business. Leaks by former National Security Agency [NSA] contractor Edward Snowden have threatened to confirm customers' worst fears about an industry that relies on monitoring and tracking the behavior of its customers—and convincing them that this kind of corporate surveillance is beneficial.

"That's part of their dangerous dance now, since the near-term economic future for all those companies, every single one of them, rests on being able to track and exploit consumer data on the Internet," says Aram Sinnreich, a digital privacy expert and professor at Rutgers University School of Communication and Information in New Brunswick, N.J. "They're not going to be able to do that if the idea of tracking has become so toxic—thanks to this pervasive government surveillance—that consumers may not be willing to abide it in a commercial context."

This year's Snowden revelations have illustrated the extent to which many of these companies have cooperated with government officials. In the NSA's PRISM program, the government gains "front-door" access to company servers under a court-approved process.

But in another top-secret document from the Snowden leaks, even company executives were startled to learn that, with another program called MUSCULAR, the NSA has broken into communication arteries that link Yahoo and Google data centers around the globe. Whereas PRISM requested specific data, this program taps into the flow of information with a virtual secret spigot.

"These companies have all cooperated with the FBI [Federal Bureau of Investigation] in national security investigations for years," says Frank Scafidi, a former 20-year veteran field agent with the FBI, now the director of public affairs at the National Insurance Crime Bureau in Sacramento, Calif. "But to learn in recent times of the government's silent vacuuming of signals and cell calls and text messages and emails— all without the knowledge of these companies or the individuals communicating through them—has raised sufficient ire to produce this reform coalition."

Even before the latest revelations, criticism had poured in from Europe and South America, especially after it was revealed that the NSA had recorded cell phone calls of German chancellor Angela Merkel.

"It's clear that pressure is increasing, especially internationally," says Professor Sinnreich. "The secondary story here

Tech Giants Against Government Surveillance

Google has spent months and millions of dollars encrypting email, search queries and other information flowing among its data centers worldwide. Facebook's chief executive said at a conference this fall that the government "blew it." And though it has not been announced publicly, Twitter plans to set up new types of encryption to protect messages from snoops.

It is all reaction to reports of how far the government has gone in spying on Internet users, sneaking around tech companies to tap into their systems without their knowledge or cooperation. . . .

When reports of surveillance by the National Security Agency surfaced in June [2013], the companies were frustrated at the exposure of their cooperation with the government in complying with lawful requests for the data of foreign users, and they scrambled to explain to customers that they had no choice but to obey the requests.

But as details of the scope of spying emerge, frustration has turned to outrage, and cooperation has turned to war.

The industry has learned that it knew of only a fraction of the spying, and it is grappling with the risks of being viewed as an enabler of surveillance of foreigners and American citizens.

Claire Cain Miller,
"Angry over U.S. Surveillance, Tech Giants Bolster Defenses,"
New York Times, *October 31, 2013.*

is that NSA surveillance is widely, and I think legitimately, perceived as an overreach of American power. And I think there's a real risk to these companies, since the fastest growing markets for these companies is overseas—the growing online middle-class consumer base in countries like China and India."

"If those consumers see these companies as instruments of American foreign power, they're going to take a really significant hit in those markets," he adds.

So it is in the best interests of these tech behemoths to get ahead of their critics, say other industry watchers. Indeed, the Snowden revelations have brought together companies that otherwise relentlessly engage in a struggle-to-corporate-death competition.

"These companies want to provide a unified front and make it appear as though they are standing up for the privacy rights of American citizens," emails Ann Bartow, professor of law at Pace Law School in White Plains, N.Y. "Even though they themselves compromise individual privacy quite dramatically."

"They want to try to outmaneuver or prevent any individual company from using privacy for competitive advantage," Professor Bartow continues. "For example, a social networking platform that actually respected privacy more than Facebook (not a very high bar) would be very appealing to many people. This group of companies is trying to set and enforce an 'industry standard' for privacy, and one that they prefer and control."

In an era when "privacy" is a relative term and user data remain central to revenue, tech companies are trying to build on the idea of "trust."

"Protecting the privacy of our users is incredibly important to Yahoo," said Marissa Mayer, CEO [chief executive officer] of Yahoo, in a statement released with the open letter. "Recent revelations about government surveillance activities have shaken the trust of our users, and it is time for the United States government to act to restore the confidence of citizens around the world."

> *"The truth is, for too long we've been content to play with our gadgets and let the geekpreneurs figure out the rest. But that's not their job; change-the-world blather notwithstanding, their job is to make money."*

Tech Giants Are Complicit in NSA Surveillance

Monika Bauerlein and Clara Jeffery

In the following viewpoint, Monika Bauerlein and Clara Jeffery argue that big tech companies such as Facebook have played an active role in the pervasive government surveillance programs now coming under intense criticism. They contend that big tech is just as responsible for the ongoing surveillance problem as the National Security Agency (NSA) and other government agencies and must now do what is necessary to cope with an environment in which citizens are much more critical about how their personal data is used. Bauerlein and Jeffery are the editors in chief of Mother Jones.

As you read, consider the following questions:

1. According to Bauerlein and Jeffery, why is user data so important to tech companies?

2. According to Bauerlein and Jeffery, what is the importance of Edward Snowden's information leak insofar as it pertained to online privacy?

3. According to Bauerlein and Jeffery, who will be most responsible for changing the way tech giants use personal data?

"That social norm is just something that has evolved over time" is how Mark Zuckerberg justified hijacking your privacy in 2010, after Facebook imperiously reset everyone's default settings to "public." "People have really gotten comfortable sharing more information and different kinds." Riiight. Little did we know that by that time, Facebook (along with Google, Microsoft, etc.) was already collaborating with the National Security Agency's [NSA's] PRISM program that swept up personal data on vast numbers of Internet users.

The Problem with Privacy

In light of what we know now, Zuckerberg's high-hat act has a bit of a creepy feel, like that guy who told you he was a documentary photographer but turned out to be a Peeping Tom. But perhaps we shouldn't be surprised: At the core of Facebook's business model is the notion that our personal information is not, well, ours. And much like the NSA, no matter how often it's told to stop using data in ways we didn't authorize, it just won't quit. Not long after Zuckerberg's "evolving norm" dodge, Facebook had to promise the feds it would stop doing things like putting your picture in ads targeted at your "friends"; that promise lasted only until this past summer, when it suddenly "clarified" its right to do with your (and your kids') photos whatever it sees fit. And just this week, Facebook analytics chief Ken Rudin told the *Wall Street Journal* that the company is experimenting with new ways to suck up your data, such as "how long a user's cursor hovers over a certain part of its website, or whether a user's newsfeed is visible at a given moment on the screen of his or her mobile phone."

There will be a lot of talk in coming months about the government surveillance golem assembled in the shadows of the Internet. Good. But what about the pervasive claim the private sector has staked to our digital lives, from where we (and our phones) spend the night to how often we text our spouse or swipe our Visa at the liquor store? It's not a stretch to say that there's a corporate spy operation equal to the NSA—indeed, sometimes it's hard to tell the difference.

Yes, Silicon Valley libertarians, we know there *is* a difference: When we hand over information to Facebook, Google, Amazon, and PayPal, we click "I Agree." We don't clear our cookies. We recycle the opt-out notice. And let's face it, that's exactly what Internet companies are trying to get us to do: hand over data without thinking of the transaction as a commercial one. It's all so casual, cheery, intimate—like, *like?*

But beyond all the Friends and Hangouts and Favorites, there's cold, hard cash, and, as they say on Sand Hill Road [a road in Menlo Park, CA, known for its concentration of venture capital companies], when the product is free, you are the product. It's your data that makes Facebook worth $100 billion and Google $300 billion. It's your data that info-mining companies like Acxiom and Datalogix package, repackage, sift, and sell. And it's your data that, as we've now learned, tech giants also pass along to the government. Let's review: Companies have given the NSA access to the records of every phone call made in the United States. Companies have inserted NSA-designed "back doors" in security software, giving the government (and, potentially, hackers—or other governments) access to everything from bank records to medical data. And oh, yeah, companies also flat-out sell your data to the NSA and other agencies.

A Changing Environment

To be sure, no one should expect a bunch of engineers and their lawyers to turn into privacy warriors. What we could have done without was the industry's pearl-clutching when the eavesdropping was finally revealed: the insistence . . . that "we have never heard of PRISM" . . . [and shocked] to discover that data mining was going on here. Only after it became undeniably clear that they had known and had cooperated did they duly hurl indignation at the NSA and the FISA court [United States Foreign Intelligence Surveillance Act Court] that approved the data demands. Heartfelt? Maybe. But it also served a branding purpose: Wait! Don't unfriend us! Kittens!

O hai, check out Mark Zuckerberg at this year's Tech-Crunch conference: The NSA really "blew it," he said, by insisting that its spying was mostly directed at foreigners. "Like, oh, wonderful, that's really going to inspire confidence in

American Internet companies. I thought that was really bad." Shorter: What matters is how quickly Facebook can achieve total world domination.

Maybe the biggest upside to l'affaire Snowden [referring to Edward Snowden's leaking of top-secret information about NSA surveillance activities] is that Americans are starting to wise up. "Advertisers" rank barely behind "hackers or criminals" on the list of entities that Internet users say they don't want to be tracked by (followed by "people from your past"). A solid majority say it's very important to control access to their email, downloads, and location data. Perhaps that's why, outside the more sycophantic crevices of the tech press, the new iPhone's biometric capability was not greeted with the unadulterated exultation of the pre-PRISM era.

The truth is, for too long we've been content to play with our gadgets and let the geekpreneurs figure out the rest. But that's not their job; change-the-world blather notwithstanding, their job is to make money. That leaves the hard stuff—like how much privacy we'll trade for either convenience or security—in someone else's hands: ours. It's our responsibility to take charge of our online behavior . . . and, more urgently, it's our job to prod our elected representatives to take on the intelligence agencies and their private-sector pals.

The NSA was able to do what it did because, post-9/11 [referring to the September 11, 2001, terrorist attacks], "with us or against us" absolutism cowed any critics of its expanding dragnet. Facebook does what it does because, unlike Europe—where both privacy and the ability to know what companies have on you are codified as fundamental rights—we haven't been conditioned to see Orwellian [referring to author George Orwell's account of the destruction of a free and open society] overreach in every algorithm. That is now changing, and both the NSA and Mark Zuckerberg will have to accept it. The social norm is evolving.

"To Pittsburgh at large, the Googlers—as they are commonly called—are living, breathing examples of the regional transformation from a blue-collar workforce built on ore to a silicon-powered center of science and technology."

Tech Companies Are Changing Communities for the Better

Mackenzie Carpenter and Deborah M. Todd

In the following viewpoint, Mackenzie Carpenter and Deborah M. Todd argue that the rise of tech giants has been highly beneficial for the cities and neighborhoods in which they have laid down roots. They point out that the arrival of Google in the Pittsburgh, Pennsylvania, neighborhood of Larimer has substantially improved the area's outlook, raising property values and encouraging economic growth, among other things. This, the authors contend, demonstrates just how much of a positive difference tech giants can make in American cities. Carpenter, a staff writer, and Todd, a small business reporter, are both contributing writers for the Pittsburgh Post-Gazette.

As you read, consider the following questions:

1. According to the viewpoint, how has Google's arrival in Larimer encouraged commercial growth in the neighborhood?

2. According to the authors, how has Google's arrival impacted the socioeconomic makeup of the surrounding neighborhoods?

3. How has Google's arrival affected property values in Pittsburgh's Eleventh Ward, according to the authors?

You can see them at the Coffee Tree Roasters at Bakery Square—scruffy Mark Zuckerberg lookalikes sauntering in for a latte, their Google badges dangling from blue lanyards. (It's not a status they care to advertise: Gaze too long and one young man tucks his lanyard under his T-shirt.)

They are the Googlers, approximately 350 of them housed in the former Nabisco factory on Penn Avenue in Larimer. Where decades ago the aroma of baking Lorna Doones wafted out the windows, now every 150 feet or so, micro-kitchens stand ready to supply free salads, Cheerios, organic protein bars and quinoa.

Soon, the local Google head count will grow to 500, maybe more.

The people who work for Google Pittsburgh have a reputation as an enigmatic mix of well-compensated, Mensa-minded, 20- to 30-something graduates of colleges for the cognitive elite. The stereotype also assumes they are mostly single hipsters who ride bikes to work and hang out at bars and restaurants like the Livermore, Spoon, Avenue B, BRGR and Social after work.

There's no denying parts of the stereotype hold true, but it's hard to tell whether it's Googlers or everyday Pittsburghers snagging booths in East Liberty restaurants. While Google's move from Carnegie Mellon University [CMU] to Bakery

Square in 2010 brought an infusion of hundreds—compared to dozens of Apple and Intel employees operating out of CMU's [Robert Mehrabian] Collaborative Innovation Center at the time—it also reinforced an existing culture in the neighborhood of hipsters and geeks who never quite fit in the city's blue-collar box.

Still, to Pittsburgh at large, the Googlers—as they are commonly called—are living, breathing examples of the regional transformation from a blue-collar workforce built on ore to a silicon-powered center of science and technology.

On a larger scale, Google has 70 offices in more than 40 countries, and just where Pittsburgh falls in that equation isn't clear to area residents eight years after the secretive California tech giant first laid its foundation in Larimer.

Tech Talent Was Already Here

More than 350,000 people live within five miles of Google Pittsburgh's offices, according to census data, and some of the region's top employers—UPMC [University of Pittsburgh Medical Center], Pitt [University of Pittsburgh] and Carnegie Mellon University—are within two miles. There's a lot of cross-pollination: A 24-hour shuttle runs between Google and CMU, where Google staffers even sit on thesis committees.

Some bristle at the notion that Pittsburgh's reputation as a high-tech magnet was only created after Google opened an office.

Carnegie Mellon had spent decades fostering some of the most brilliant computer scientists and software engineers in the world, so it only makes sense that companies would be drawn here to harness that brainpower for commerce, said Andrew Moore, founder of the original Google Pittsburgh office. The British-born, Cambridge-educated computer scientist came to CMU in 1993, joined Google in 2006 and recently returned to the university as dean of the School of Computer Science.

"When I relocate people, it's not all about CMU or Google," he said. "They ask, 'What else is going on? What other interesting, exciting things are there to do?'"

In 2001—the year *Wikipedia* and Apple iTunes were launched—Google had already become the largest search engine in the world. By 2005, it was wooing CMU's Mr. Moore—developer of ingenious advertising search software—and other engineers to come to its headquarters in Mountain View, Calif.

Mr. Moore didn't go to the mountain, as it were, so the mountain came to Mr. Moore, hiring him and opening its first office at CMU. In 2010, Google moved into 40,000 square feet at the newly developed Bakery Square.

Actually, Mr. Moore hates being cited as the reason Google came to Pittsburgh.

"You can write that I stormed angrily out of the room when asked that question," the affable engineer said in an interview in Carnegie Mellon's Gates Center for Computer Science. "There were some very good people involved in this from the beginning," he said, adding that CMU and Google remain very close.

Google is fiercely protective of its turf, even when it comes to CMU.

When Luis von Ahn sold the first game that he'd developed at Carnegie Mellon to Google—the ESP Game—the company wouldn't permit a news release mentioning the university at all.

So when Mr. von Ahn sold reCAPTCHA, the human recognition technology he developed at CMU, to the search engine giant in 2009, he had it written into the contract that Carnegie Mellon could issue its own news release.

"They have their own strategic reasons for wanting to say this or that," said Mr. von Ahn, 35, of Shadyside. His digital company Duolingo, a language teaching app, employs 40 people—many of them former Google employees. (Duolingo was Apple's best free iPhone app of 2013 and was among the best on Google Play as well.)

CMU is to Google and the rest of the city's tech companies what, perhaps, iron ore factories were to the steel industry in the 19th century, suggested Pittsburgh mayor Bill Peduto.

"Andrew Carnegie decided to locate in Pittsburgh because he had rivers and rails to get the materials to build his products and get them to market," said Mr. Peduto. "This new economy is not under that same structure. Google is not looking to locate next to a highway. They don't need an infrastructure of raw materials. CMU and Pitt are the factories churning out that talent."

If You Build It, They Will Come

Today, at 160,000 square feet, Google is the largest tenant at Bakery Square. . . .

The rise in talent concentrated in the neighborhood has helped fuel a rise in commercial growth. A Target store opened at the intersection formerly known as Penn Circle in 2011, high-end boutiques joined the newly constructed Broad Street development Indigo Square and a $23 million renovation is now transforming a former YMCA into the Ace Hotel—a boutique chain rumored to be a favorite among Googlers worldwide.

Besides small to medium organizations such as TechShop, which President Barack Obama visited earlier this year [2014], the neighborhood also has drawn in start-up incubator/accelerator Thrill Mill and co-working spaces such as Beauty Shoppe.

But is that a direct result of Google, or just coincidence?

Lori Moran, president of the East Liberty Quarter Chamber of Commerce, said Google is helping to accelerate commercial and residential growth that had been on the rise, in fits and starts, since 2000, when Home Depot set up shop on Highland Avenue.

"Google's entrance into this market has helped focus a national spotlight on East Liberty," Ms. Moran said.

When Google came in, it brought more spending power and a less conservative population, she said.

One direct spin-off from Google is Vanessa Jameson.

The East Liberty resident and mother of a 2-year-old had worked for Google since 2007, first in the Bay Area and then moving to the Pittsburgh office in 2011 to be closer to family. She decided to start her own company, developing a mobile app that would allow mothers to network with other mothers. After getting funding from South Side–based start-up investment fund Innovation Works, she left Google to oversee what will be an app called Covey—as in a group of birds.

"I'm an interesting case," she said. "I joke about how I did it all backwards."

Meanwhile, over at CMU, Apple, Intel, Caterpillar and Disney have all established or increased their own Pittsburgh profile—not necessarily because of Google, said Terri Glueck, spokeswoman for Innovation Works.

"There's no real cause and effect. You can't directly say that when Google moved here that's when things took off, but it is relational. They're part of a rising tide that is making Google better, Pittsburgh better and start-ups better," said Ms. Glueck, noting that venture capital investment dollars peaked in 2010 at $205 million, slipping a bit in 2011 and 2012 but recovering in 2013. This year promises to set new local records. For the first nine months of 2014, the region attracted $250 million in venture capital, already well beyond the amount raised in 2010.

And the local tech industry's growth hasn't just been seen in the East End, Ms. Glueck said. There's 4moms, in the Strip District, which got $41 million in venture capital; NoWait, in

Oakland, $10 million; the Resumator, in the North Hills, $15 million; and Complexa, on the South Side, $10 million.

In high-tech "innovative" cultures, hopping from one firm to another is a sign of desirability, not failure, Mr. Peduto noted.

"In the past, you worked for one firm and if you wanted to advance, you had to leave Pittsburgh. Now, you have the ability to work at one company and do parallel advancement at another and that is going to build off itself," he said.

Sparking Development

Another spin-off from Google could be the robust growth in housing prices in the East End.

But while real estate agent Elizabeth Swartz has helped several Google families settle in the city, not all do. One client chose O'Hara, and she knows of other Googlers who have bought houses in the suburbs.

Pittsburgh's appeal to Googlers or transplants working for other tech companies from California or Boston "is the affordability, the ability to have a single-income family where only one spouse has to work. The schools are also a deciding factor, and for some, that tends to mean the suburbs," she said.

Then again, Cindy Ingram, a real estate agent with Coldwell Banker, sold a house in Squirrel Hill to a Googler for nearly $800,000. "They want to bike to work, they love the parks, they're interested in the public schools—and they don't talk about their jobs. I spent six months with one client and I never did find out what he did at Google," she said.

It might make sense that a lot of Google employees would move in across Penn Avenue into Bakery Square 2.0, located where the mostly windowless 1970s-era Reizenstein middle school, later the Pittsburgh Barack Obama Academy of International Studies, stood until it was demolished in early 2013.

The new apartment building is part of a mixed-use complex called Bakery Living that will include a 218,000-square-foot office building and more apartments. So far, the first building is 90 percent occupied, with only a few one-bedroom units left, said Todd Reidbord, co-owner of Shadyside-based Walnut Capital, which developed Bakery Square and Bakery Living.

How many new Google employees working in the new LEED [Leadership in Energy and Environmental Design]–certified office tower will take a short walk home to a Bakery Living space?

According to a survey by Walnut Capital this past summer, only 4 percent of residents of the new apartment complex work at Google. Thirteen percent work at UPMC, 6 percent at Pitt, 3 percent at AGH [Allegheny General Hospital], 3 percent at CMU and 71 percent are categorized as "other."

Most of the residents—57 percent—come from other states, 32 percent from the city, 8 percent from Pennsylvania, 1 percent from western Pennsylvania and 2 percent from foreign countries.

The "luxury" apartments are relatively spare, but the idea is to encourage social activity downstairs in the soaring, two-story lobby, said Gregg Perelman, Mr. Reidbord's partner at Walnut Capital, which makes sense given that 58 percent of the residents are in their 20s and another 26 percent are in their 30s.

Walnut Capital was by no means the pioneer in drawing young professionals and families to the neighborhood. Lots of people, starting with former mayor Tom Murphy, who lured Home Depot to East Liberty, can take credit for the neighborhood's rebirth.

Then there's Molly Blasier, a developer based in Point Breeze who identified properties in 1998 along Centre Avenue that she thought could make a perfect site for a Whole Foods Market. She contacted the grocery company and partnered

Tech and the City

The urban shift in venture capital and high-tech start-ups has implications that go way beyond jobs and economic development. By their very presence, they will enhance cities' already considerable prowess at problem solving, helping them function as laboratories for solutions to the most pressing social and environmental problems of the day—from energy and pollution to affordable housing, better schooling, and reduced crime.

Cities aren't just the location of innovative enterprises—they are innovation machines in their own right, uniquely equipped to generate solutions to the problems that they create, a virtuous circle if ever there were one.

Richard Florida, "The Urban Tech Revolution,"
Urban Land, *October 7, 2013.*

with Steve Mosites Jr. of the Mosites Co. to bring Whole Foods here in 2002 as part of Eastside I.

The entrance of the high-end grocer was one of the first signs of the neighborhood's pending demographic shift. Within the next few years, East Liberty's East Mall, Liberty Park and Penn Circle High Rise complexes were razed and replaced with new housing developments and businesses, including the Target complex that rerouted the course of what was once Penn Circle.

Over the next two years, another Mosites project, Eastside III, is slated to emerge with more than 360 housing units and 40,000 square feet of retail space.

A lot of this kind of development would have happened anyway, given the growth of the neighborhood. "But Google certainly helps," Mr. Reidbord said.

A Real Estate Boom

With hundreds of units of subsidized and mixed-income projects in the pipeline, East Liberty is maintaining a balance that, so far, also makes room for families with a range of incomes, although in nearby neighborhoods—Highland Park and North Point Breeze, for example—there are stories of large sums being paid for single-family homes by Google employees or other beneficiaries of the East End's high-tech boom.

A Highland Park resident who moved to the neighborhood three years ago from the suburbs has seen that happening firsthand, noting that a boarded-up house next door was bought by a real estate agent for $70,000, who then spent $150,000 renovating it. The day the newly renovated house was put on the market, it was bought at asking price for $450,000 by a Google employee, said the resident, a local business executive who declined to be identified.

County assessment figures back up the residents' claims. One parcel in the 800 block of Highland Avenue that sold for $165,000 in 1998 went for $310,000 last year. Two blocks over in the 1200 block of Farragut Street, a home valued at $307,400 this year sold for $520,000 in July.

While Google and Bakery Square sit firmly inside the neighborhood of Larimer for city planning purposes, East Liberty and other surrounding communities may be the ones that have benefited most from the tech giant's presence.

The city's 11th Ward—which encompasses a large part of East Liberty, Highland Park and Morningside—saw housing prices nearly double from an average of $100,835 in 2005 to an average of $198,357 as of Nov. 17, according to South Side–based real estate information service RealSTATs.

In the 8th Ward—containing portions of East Liberty, Friendship and Bloomfield—sale prices jumped from an average of $105,061 in 2005 to $177,439 during the same period.

The 7th Ward, home to portions of Shadyside and Point Breeze, saw home sales sail from an average of $249,086 in 2005 to an average of $352,322 in that span of time.

The 12th Ward—home to Lincoln-Lemington, Belmar and Larimer—didn't fare as well: Average sale prices dropped from $34,880 in 2005 to $31,694 as of Nov. 17.

As real estate in the East End's formerly depressed areas continues to percolate, Google's presence at what might be just another upscale mall has added cachet for customers who patronize Social, a bar/restaurant at Bakery Square frequented not just by Google employees but locals interested in soaking up the atmosphere—one augmented by the sight of people coding at their computers while sitting at the bar.

"Google definitely ups the coolness factor," said Ryan Teeder, 25, who was sipping a craft beer at one of Social's outdoor tables on a warm August evening. He had actually come to pick up his 14-year-old brother Ross, who had spent the afternoon at TechShop. "I live in White Oak, but when I come here, I feel like I'm in Brooklyn or some other really cool place where all the action is."

Bobby Fry, a co-owner of the South Highland Avenue craft cocktail bar the Livermore, agrees. "They're very interesting and interested in things outside their day job," said Mr. Fry, who opened his establishment 18 months ago and now serves 1,500 people a week, many of them from Google. "They give more atmosphere to the place."

"We've become really good friends with people in the start-up community, including Google, but also folks at these awesome coworking spaces that have sprung up around the neighborhood," he said.

As he spoke, he was in the process of planning a live podcast from the bar that night with Serge Smailbegovic, one of the founders of Thrill Mill, an early incubator start-up and a neighbor of Google's.

The podcast was going to be about Mr. Smailbegovic's new app, which will provide "an alternative way to order food from your seat at baseball games," he said.

And no, the app is not a Google product, but Google's very presence has given smaller entrepreneurs the confidence to come in and start something new, said Mr. Fry, 29, who's also a co-owner of Bar Marco in The Strip—another Googler hangout.

"So far, so good," he said. "I'll take it."

> "By pushing poor and working-class people to the suburbs, gentrification doesn't benefit everyone. Instead, it reconfigures the geographic lines of racial and economic inequality."

Tech Companies Are Causing Gentrification

Adam Hudson

In the following viewpoint, Adam Hudson argues that the ever increasing presence of tech companies in San Francisco is leading to an extreme, harmful pattern of gentrification within the city. He contends that the massive influx of affluent tech workers is pushing low-income families and minorities out of neighborhoods they have called home for generations. In short, he claims that tech gentrification is oppressing the less fortunate for the benefit of the wealthy. Hudson is a reporting fellow with Truthout.

As you read, consider the following questions:

1. According to Kalima Rose, what steps are involved in the process of gentrification?

2. According to Hudson, how is the gentrification of San Francisco leading to a trend toward suburbanization in the city?

3. According to Hudson, how is the gentrification of San Francisco a microcosm of what is happening in cities around the United States?

On January 21 [2014], dozens of protesters, decrying displacement and inequality, gathered near City Hall in San Francisco on a chilly Tuesday morning. At around 9:15 A.M., they marched down Market Street and blockaded two tech shuttles, one that was parked at a MUNI (San Francisco Municipal Railway) bus stop, the other in the middle of the street. Tech shuttles—also infamously known as "Google buses"—are private corporate buses that take tech industry workers from their homes in San Francisco down the peninsula to work in Silicon Valley.

Protesters surrounded the buses and placed signs near them that read: "Stop Displacement Now" and "Warning: Rents and Evictions Up Near Private Shuttle Stops." A UC [University of California]-Berkeley study and maps show that evictions and rent increases often follow the locations of tech bus stops. One sign bluntly read: "F--- off Google."

Present at the protest was Martina Ayala, a teacher, artist and consultant for San Francisco nonprofits working with low-income families. She is currently facing a no-fault eviction from her residence in San Francisco's Outer Richmond neighborhood that sits next to the Pacific Ocean beach. Ayala told Truthout, "The landlord would like us to self-evict"—but not by way of a buyout, in which landlords evict tenants by paying them to leave. Instead, Ayala said, "They're trying to get us out without having to pay the eviction costs. And so they're doing that by harassing us and calling us every day, sending us three-day notices to pay rent or quit without following through with service." Why would the landlord go to such lengths to push the family out? Ayala says, "Even though we are paying $1,750, that is still not enough for the landlord, because the average rent is now $3,000."

The Google bus blockade lasted for a half hour. Afterward, the crowd marched down Grove Street to the San Francisco Association of Realtors, then ended at City Hall. Much of the media coverage of the protest focused on the Google bus blockade. However, the protesters emphasized that the tech industry was not the only culprit. Developers, real estate brokers, and City Hall all play a role in economically displacing many San Francisco residents.

Not all protesters were mad at the tech workers riding the buses. Some encouraged tech workers to support the protesters' cause. One sign read, "Get Off the Bus, Join Us!"

A few hours after the protest, swarms of residents, tech industry workers and reporters packed themselves inside City Hall to attend a San Francisco Municipal Transportation Agency (SFMTA) hearing about starting a pilot program to have tech shuttles pay $1 each time they use a MUNI bus stop. It is against city law for others to block MUNI bus stops. Violators have to pay a $271 fine. MUNI bus riders pay $2 per ride. People who ride the bus and don't pay bus fare face a $100 fine. Poor people and people of color are often targeted by transit agents and police for not paying fare. Tech bus riders, on the other hand, do not face such penalties.

The hearing was divided by tech industry workers, who largely supported the plan, and residents who felt it wasn't enough to curb the deeper problem of displacement. At the hearing, Roberto Hernandez of Our Mission No Eviction, a San Francisco resident born and raised in the Mission District, said, "Children are getting to school late because of these tech buses that roll through the Mission. They're late, and they don't eat breakfast. So they're there with an empty stomach. They start in school late because they're getting to school late." Rodriguez told Truthout he had no problem with tech workers, but felt the $1 fee plan was an "insult" and "had no involvement of the community at all. We're concerned about the impact that these buses are having." He added, "If you ride a MUNI bus, it's slow; it's late; it stinks. Now you ride one of those [tech] buses, you get Wi-Fi; you get luxury on that bus; you get everything. But those buses, for us, is just a symbol of what rich folks can get away with." After about three to four hours of discussion, the city approved the pilot program. The next month, after pressure from community activists and organizations like People Organized to Win Employment Rights (POWER), Google agreed to donate $6.8 million over the next two years to fund free MUNI passes for low- and middle-income youth.

Two weeks after the tech shuttle hearing was the San Francisco tenants' convention, where hundreds of city residents and leaders gathered in an elementary school cafeteria to propose solutions to fix the city's housing problem. San Francisco supervisor David Campos, who represents the Mission District, attended the convention to show support for the growing movement. "Right now, the middle class in San Francisco is being pushed out. It's becoming a city that only millionaires can afford, and you see here that there is a groundswell across the city that people are saying, 'We're not gonna let that happen anymore. We want a city that is affordable for all of us.'"

Also at the convention was Tyler Macmillan, the executive director of the Eviction Defense Collaborative (EDC), a nonprofit legal services clinic that assists residents facing eviction lawsuits from landlords. He told Truthout how the city's judicial system works against eviction victims. "The vast majority of laws are written by and for folks who own property," said Macmillan. "So when you fight to defend evictions, you face a code of civil procedure, the civil code, even elements of our local law that really favor folks who are wealthy and who have access to good attorneys. And so for most tenants in San Francisco, both of those things are missing. They don't have money to get to an attorney, and then they're dealing with a set of laws that are really, especially at the state level, against them in terms of the rights of property."

To evict a tenant, landlords give them a three-day notice to pay rent or leave. If neither happens, then the landlord can file a lawsuit to evict. Tenants are given a five-day summons to appear in court, which is barely enough time to get a lawyer and prepare oneself to fight an arduous legal battle. Moreover, most judges are property owners and landlords. As a result, "they come in with the assumption that the tenant is wrong," says Macmillan.

A New Wave of Gentrification

San Francisco is experiencing a wave of unprecedented hyper-gentrification and urban removal. The city was gentrified [changing an old neighborhood by improving it and making it more appealing to people who have money] before, and has long been a pricey place, but this current episode is more extreme than previous ones.

San Francisco rent has skyrocketed to obscene levels. Median rent in San Francisco is over $3,000 a month, with some neighborhoods in the $4,000–$5,000 range. Average rent is in the same range. Even rooms for $1,000 a month are virtually nonexistent. Rents in 2013 increased over 10 percent from the previous year, which is more than three times higher than the national average of 3 percent. This makes San Francisco perhaps the least affordable city for middle-class families in the country, with New York City following closely behind. It's so expensive that even San Francisco's minimum wage, which is the highest in the country at over $10 an hour, is barely enough to live. One would have to work five, six, or more minimum-wage jobs to make the city's rent. Moreover, San Francisco is one of the most unequal urban areas, and its income inequality is growing the fastest in the nation.

Evictions have also shot up, displacing hundreds of San Francisco residents. According to the Anti-Eviction Mapping Project, a grassroots project that has been counting and mapping evictions in San Francisco, "The number of evictions in 2013 has surpassed evictions in 2006, the height of the real estate bubble. Total no-fault evictions are up 17 percent compared to 2006. More significantly, there has been a 115 percent increase in total evictions since last year" in 2012. From 1997 to 2013, there have been over 11,000 no-fault evictions—either through demolition, owner move-in, or the Ellis Act. The Ellis Act is a California state law that allows landlords to evict tenants to "go out of business" by pulling their property off the market. This allows speculators to swoop in and flip the property. In fact, speculators are driving many Ellis Act evictions. The Anti-Eviction Mapping Project reports that Ellis Act evictions "increased by 175 percent" in 2013 "compared to the year before." Additionally, "Demolitions have gone from 45 in 2006 to 134 in 2013, a 197 percent increase."

The displacement of San Francisco's African American population was the canary in the coal mine for today's current incarnation of gentrification. Previous waves of gentrification and urban renewal, particularly in neighborhoods like the Fillmore District, which is famous for its historic jazz scene and was long known as the "Harlem of the West," exiled many African Americans from San Francisco. According to census figures, in 1970, African Americans constituted 13.4 percent of the city's population. In 1980, they dropped to 12.7 percent; then to 10.9 percent in 1990. By 2000, African Americans made up 7.8 percent of the city's population. Now, San Francisco's black population hovers around 5 percent or 6 percent only.

Willie Ratcliff, publisher of *San Francisco Bay View* newspaper, told Truthout, "San Francisco has certainly conspired to drive us [African Americans] out of here" through racially discriminatory practices in the economic and criminal justice systems. "Particularly, what they do in San Francisco, they send black people to prison and [provide] no jobs." While they are 6 percent of the city's population, African Americans constitute 56 percent of San Francisco jail inmates. Unemployment for black San Franciscans has remained high for a while. For black youth, unemployment is 19.4 percent, while it is 4.8 percent for the city. African Americans are also disproportionately impacted by evictions in San Francisco, as they are 29 percent of EDC's clients for eviction lawsuits, according to the group's studies.

The wave is so severe that nonprofits and organizations that help marginalized communities are struggling to finance their offices in San Francisco. Homeless Youth Alliance, which helped homeless youth for over a decade, closed last Christmas because it could not afford rent. To fix this, the city plans to "spend $4.5 million to assist nonprofits facing eviction or struggling to make rent," according to the *San Francisco Examiner*.

As the poor and middle classes are pushed out of the city, San Francisco welcomes the booming tech industry, whose workers' average salaries are over $100,000. In April 2011, with a push from Mayor Ed Lee, the San Francisco Board of Supervisors passed a city ordinance that gives Twitter and other tech companies a 1.5 percent city payroll tax cut for the next six years in return for those businesses staying in San Francisco's mid–Market Street area. The tax breaks must be reapproved every year. In 2012, the tax cuts cost the city $1.9 million and were reapproved for this year. Twitter is expected to get $22 million from the tax break over six years and possibly more since stock options are untaxed, and the company is now publicly traded. Twitter's IPO [initial public offering] is also expected to create more millionaires.

In exchange for tax breaks, San Francisco's tech companies have to make charitable contributions to the city known as community benefit agreements (CBAs). But those contributions largely benefit other members of the tech industry. They include Yelp reviews, cocktail parties and employee-only ballet performances. Contributions are made at the company's whim, and there is no enforcement mechanism to ensure they help the community. Meanwhile, community members have yet to see anything meaningful come from the CBAs.

Some argue that San Francisco's housing problem stems from a lack of supply. If the city built more housing, the argument goes, rent would come down, but the city makes it difficult to build. However, San Francisco has had a building boom since 2012, and rent has increased instead of decreased. San Francisco's chief economist Ted Egan said that to noticeably reduce rental prices, the city would have to build 100,000 market-rate units—the same amount it's built since the 1920s. Mayor Ed Lee, meanwhile, has proposed to build 30,000 housing units by 2020. Building 100,000 market-rate units would have the same impact on affordability as giving every low-income household—about 56,000 in the city—$75,000 to assist their down payments, according to Egan. Unless San Francisco is willing to build an extremely high amount, building more housing would hardly reduce rental costs. Additionally, while building more housing is not bad, the issue is what kind. As *Uptown Almanac*'s Jackson West points out, "even if you remove the permitting costs from the process, it's not profitable to build anything but luxury housing." This raises the question—who is this development for?

The Process of Gentrification

Whenever the term "gentrification" is thrown around, confusion often follows. Director Spike Lee went on an expletive-laden rant against gentrification in New York City, saying, "You can't do that. You can't just come in the neighborhood and start bogarting and say, like you're motherf-----' Columbus and kill off the Native Americans. Or what they do in Brazil, what they did to the indigenous people. You have to come with respect. There's a code. There's people." In response, columnist Joshua Greenman wrote in the *New York Daily News*, "But Americans of all races, motivated by economic and cultural currents, have moved from city to city, and from neighborhood to neighborhood, since civilization began.... Everyone replaces someone. Sometimes, neighborhoods go from predominantly Latino and African-American to increasingly white." Greenman's characterization is fairly common—gentrification is typically portrayed as a natural, benign process of people simply moving from one neighborhood to another. Depicted this way, challenges to gentrification seem dyspeptic and naive. However, gentrification does not occur inevitably. It is a systematic process with many moving parts.

As a process, gentrification is typically preceded by disinvestment in predominantly black and brown neighborhoods. A new report by Causa Justa:: Just Cause (CJJC), a Bay Area tenants' rights organization, notes that investment, including real estate development and infrastructure funding, usually follows white populations while shying away from communities of color, according to an *In These Times* summary. For decades, banks denied financial services, such as loans and credit, to predominantly black and brown neighborhoods—a practice known as redlining. This generated low property values in those communities and deteriorated the neighborhoods. Then the process of displacement begins.

Kalima Rose, a senior director at PolicyLink in Oakland, California, wrote that gentrification occurs "in a series of recognizable stages." The first "involves some significant public or nonprofit redevelopment investment and/or private newcomers buying and rehabbing vacant units" in usually working-class, black and Latino neighborhoods with low property values. Next, "the neighborhood's low housing costs and other amenities become known, and housing costs rise. Displacement begins as landlords take advantage of rising market values and evict longtime residents to rent or sell to the more affluent. Increasingly, newcomers are more likely to be homeowners, and the rising property values cause down payment requirements to increase. With new residents, come commercial amenities that serve higher income levels." Then as "rehabilitation becomes more apparent, prices escalate and displacement occurs in force. New residents have lower tolerance for existing social service facilities that serve homeless populations or other low-income needs, as well as industrial and other uses they view as undesirable. Original residents are displaced along with their industries, commercial enterprises, faith institutions and cultural traditions."

In short, gentrification is trickle-down economics applied to urban development: the idea being that as long as a neighborhood is made suitable for rich and predominantly white people, the benefits will trickle down to everyone else.

Police Crack Down on Poor, Homeless

To make way for this new wave of gentrification, San Francisco police have enforced the city's criminalization efforts against the poor, homeless and working-class people of color. Last September, SFPD [San Francisco Police Department] shut down a group of chess games, claiming it was a "public nuisance" and "disguise" for drug use and gambling. This is despite it being a 30-year tradition that has helped poor people; while criminal elements often came not because of players themselves, but from surrounding unsavory characters.

Last November, "DJ" Paris Williams, a 21-year-old African American City College of San Francisco student and bicyclist, was stopped and brutalized by two undercover police officers outside his Valencia Gardens apartment in the Mission District, a historically working-class Latino neighborhood experiencing intense gentrification. The cops' issue with DJ was his riding his bike on the sidewalk near his home since the complex is private property. As he entered his home, the police

San Francisco, Tech Giants, and Gentrification

Few cities have seen as much disruption as San Francisco has over the last 10 years. Once a hotbed of progressive political activism and engagement, the city is being re-made in the image of the booming tech industry, head-quartered in Silicon Valley to the south.

Rents in some of San Francisco's most desirable neighborhoods have doubled in a year. Apartment construction has exploded in order to absorb the new residents.

The local government has embraced the disruption. Longtime residents, meanwhile, talk about fleeing or saving their city as though a hurricane is coming. But the hurricane has landed.

Susie Cagle, "The Dark Side of Startup City,"
Grist, July 26, 2013.

grabbed DJ from behind and beat him. When three residents came to help DJ, they were beaten up, too. One person, Orlando Rodriguez, had his face smashed to the ground by police and was badly bloodied.

This one incident is part of a larger trend. Bay Area hip-hop journalist Davey D reported, "As more white folks have been moving in, many black and brown folks, who long made up the majority of folks living in the Mission, have noted they are frequently being profiled and stopped by police. They are often viewed suspiciously, even though they have lived there for generations. Many feel that they are being made to feel unwelcome in their own neighborhoods, and police harassment is part of a larger process to make it so uncomfortable that folks move out."

Recently, months after DJ's assault, SFPD shot and killed 28-year-old Latino Alejandro "Alex" Nieto in Bernal Heights Park. Nieto was a City College of San Francisco scholarship student and resident of San Francisco's Bernal Heights neighborhood—south of the Mission—with hopes of becoming a youth probation officer. Police mistook Nieto's Taser for a gun. Nieto wore a Taser for his job as a nightclub security guard. SFPD dispatch audio reveals that Nieto was not acting erratically nor fired at officers before he was killed. Community members were outraged at Nieto's killing. They protested and connected his murder to the city's deepening gentrification. Nieto's family is now suing the city, claiming the killing was unjustified.

At the corner of 16th and Mission Streets in the Mission District, groups of poor and homeless people, artists, activists, sometimes drug dealers, and other passers-by regularly congregate. In response, a shady campaign called "Clean Up the Plaza" was born. The campaign was announced in June 2013, and San Francisco police began daily patrols in September, leading to increased harassment of homeless people and residents in the area. In October, Maximus Real Estate Partners submitted a proposal to the San Francisco planning commission to build a 10-story, 351-unit housing development at the 16th and Mission intersection that would cost around $175 million and replace several businesses in the area. Many community members oppose the plan. "This proposed plan doesn't take into consideration the affordable housing needs this neighborhood has," CJJC organizer Maria Zamudio told *El Tecolote*.

The 16th and Mission intersection has not always been a safe environment. However, some community members feel threatened not just by local crime, but also by police—Nieto's shooting being one reason for that. A group of activists called Coffee Not Cops, inspired by Books Not Bombs, congregate at the intersection every other Sunday to serve coffee, pastries, literature and talk to people (except police) in the area about the police presence and gentrification. On their flyer, they pose an interesting question, "Let's say crime stops on 16th and Mission. Do we really think it will be Latino families, working-class people, and young people of color who will be around to enjoy this supposed lack of crime?"

For a while, almost no one knew who was behind the "Clean Up the Plaza" campaign, and it was rumored to be linked to the planned development. It turns out that link is San Francisco political consultant Jack Davis, who has a long record of working on behalf of real estate interests and whose roommate, Gil Chavez, runs the "Clean Up the Plaza" website. Independent journalist Julia Carrie Wong confirmed that "Davis is also working as a paid consultant for the condo project at 16th and Mission."

Adding insult to injury, San Francisco is literally washing away its homeless population. Last September, the San Francisco Department of Public Works [DPW] launched a pilot program to keep the streets clean. A DPW spokeswoman told Al Jazeera America, "We wash the streets using disinfectant and steamers as part of our alleys program. We also pick up litter, human waste and other debris." But under this program, street cleaners have sprayed their high-powered hoses at homeless people sleeping on the streets. A hidden camera from the Coalition on Homelessness captured a DPW worker kicking a homeless person and trucks spraying the homeless with their powerful hoses. It is also very common to see homeless people lying on the street in downtown San Francisco, particularly along Market Street near where tech companies like Twitter are located.

Suburbanization of Poverty

Often overlooked in stories about tech buses and displacement in San Francisco is how gentrification perpetuates the suburbanization of Bay Area poverty. US census data show that, from the years 2007 to 2011, large chunks of San Francisco's middle class moved to Alameda and Contra Costa counties in the East Bay, along with other parts of California and out of state. Macmillan told Truthout that, after being evicted, many Eviction Defense Collaborative clients move to the East Bay area, including "inner and way outside of Contra Costa County." Low- and middle-income residents, many of whom are people of color who can no longer afford to live in San Francisco or Oakland, usually move to outer East Bay area suburbs like Vallejo, Antioch, and Fairfield—or as far as Stockton.

Lines of racial and class inequality lie not just in San Francisco and Oakland but also in working-class suburbs like Antioch, Pittsburg and Vallejo. Some of these cities are low to moderate income and have sizable African American and Latino populations. Pittsburg, an East Bay industrial town flanking the Sacramento River delta that connects to the San Francisco Bay, is 17.7 percent black, 42.4 percent Latino, 15.6 percent Asian, has a median household income of $58,063, and its poverty rate is 17.1 percent, according to census data. It is also home to an old coal mine, the steel company USS-POSCO [Industries] and Dow Chemical [Company]. Vallejo is 22.1 percent black, 24.9 percent Asian, and 22.6 percent Latino, has a similar median household income and a 16 percent poverty rate.

In January 2012, the Federal Reserve Bank of San Francisco released a report that analyzed the increasing poverty in Bay Area suburbs. Looking at census data, between 2000 and 2009, poverty increased in both urban and suburban areas. However, poverty rose faster in the suburbs than in urban areas and varied across racial groups. According to the report, "The number of people living in poverty rose 16 percent in the suburbs, compared to 7 percent in urban areas. Blacks and Hispanics saw the greatest percentage growth in suburban poverty, as did the native-born population." African Americans were the "only group to see a decline in the number of poor urban residents. While the number of poor blacks living in urban tracts decreased by 11 percent, the number of poor blacks in the suburbs increased by about 20 percent." San Francisco and Oakland both have declining black populations.

Poverty rose in cities like Pittsburg, Antioch, Concord, Vallejo, the fringe of San Jose and Millbrae. The percentage of poor people living in the suburbs increased among all racial groups, but the highest change was among African Americans. "The share of the poor black population living in the suburbs increased more than 7 percentage points, whereas the next highest group, Asians, increased 2 percentage points," the report said.

The report notes that several factors contributed to the suburbanization of Bay Area poverty. One is the collapse of the housing bubble in the late 2000s, which particularly hurt Stockton, Antioch and much of east Contra Costa County. In the mid-2000s, the housing boom provided affordable housing in the suburbs. Once it burst, home values dropped, foreclosures skyrocketed, people lost their jobs, and poverty increased.

Some low-income residents moved from the cities to suburbs to escape crime and find better opportunities. But gentrification also factored in suburbanizing poverty. The report notes, "The rising value of properties in the urban core may have led to indirect displacement, as landlords converted rental units to condominiums and tenancies in common (TICs), or raised the rents to the extent allowed by local regulation. Displaced residents may have moved from central cities to more affordable suburban areas."

These Bay Area working-class suburbs provide cheaper housing, some of which is Section 8. However, there are disadvantages to living in these communities. Social services that help low-income people are typically located in urban areas, where much of the poor have long been concentrated, while the suburbs lack them. Thus, poor people in the suburbs have little access to nonprofits and organizations that can help them. Moreover, Bay Area suburbs are no different than other suburbs when it comes to lacking public transportation. Bay Area Rapid Transit (BART) goes throughout much of Oakland and San Francisco but barely reaches Pittsburg and doesn't even touch Vallejo. Thus, low-income workers are forced to endure long commutes on the freeway, which leads to greater traffic and pollution.

Taken together, what's going on in San Francisco is deeper than just a fight between well-to-do tech workers and longtime San Francisco residents. San Francisco is a microcosm of what's going on in metropolitan areas around the world. From San Francisco to New York City to London, urban areas are being redesigned into playgrounds for the very rich. The poor, working and almost nonexistent middle-class people who can't afford to live in these rich Elysiums are forced to live farther away, with few resources to support themselves.

By pushing poor and working-class people to the suburbs, gentrification doesn't benefit everyone. Instead, it reconfigures the geographic lines of racial and economic inequality, granting improvements to the lives of the moneyed classes, at the expense of the needs—and sometimes, even the survival—of everyone else.

> "Apple's recent purchase of 36,000 acres of forest is just the latest in the company's growing sustainability work that includes philanthropy, clean energy, toxics reduction, and now conservation."

Tech Giants Can Be Environmentally Friendly

Tate Williams

In the following viewpoint, Tate Williams reports that big tech companies can be environmentally friendly. Focusing on Apple's efforts to go green, Williams argues that tech giants can do things to reduce their environmental footprint and play an important role in the move to change the way we treat the world around us. Williams is a Boston-based writer and editor who specializes in science, the environment, and culture. His work has appeared on websites and in publications such as Inside Philanthropy, American Forests *magazine, and* mental_floss.

As you read, consider the following questions:

1. According to Williams, why might it seem surprising that Apple is now considered an environmental leader?

2. What has Apple done to become an environmental leader, according to the viewpoint?

3. According to Williams, why was Steve Jobs not as effective as a leader when it came to the environment as Tim Cook?

Apple's recent purchase of 36,000 acres of forest is just the latest in the company's growing sustainability work that includes philanthropy, clean energy, toxics reduction, and now conservation. Can Tim Cook prove that a huge corporation going green is more than lip service?

Green Apple

If you had told most environmentalists even five years ago that Apple would become an environmental leader, it would have been a hard sell. In 2011, Greenpeace rated the company the least green based on its data centers' energy mix. The company regularly came under fire for lack of transparency about its carbon footprint and pollution in its supply chain. And Steve Jobs for years—at least publicly—was disengaged with philanthropy and sustainability.

How times have changed, and quickly. Last week [in April 2015], Apple announced that it would purchase two large tracts of "working forest" to be handed over to the Conservation Fund for sustainable management and pulp production. The company stated that the paper produced by the forests is equivalent to about half of the non-recycled paper that Apple used in its packaging last year. Apple's goal is to hit 100 percent. But that's just one of the steps the company has taken:

- Lisa Jackson, former head of the EPA [Environmental Protection Agency] under [Barack] Obama joined the company in 2013 as Apple's vice president of environmental initiatives.

- The company's U.S. facilities and data centers are all now powered by clean energy, and 87 percent of global operations are. Apple is now at the top of the Greenpeace ranking that it flunked in 2011.

- The company is spending $848 million on a solar plant in California, and announced recently it would be investing in another solar project in China.

- The company has been ahead of others in phasing out certain toxic chemicals used in production.

- Tim Cook has become a highly vocal environmental advocate, calling climate change the issue of his generation and saying the time for debate has passed.

Cook has become a force in philanthropy and a public social activist as well. He said in a recent interview with *Fortune* that he would be giving all of his wealth away—that's close to $800 million worth of Apple stock. Under Cook, Apple has fired up new philanthropic endeavors, including donating to support employees' volunteer hours and donation matching. And perhaps most well received, he came out publicly as gay and slammed homophobic legislation appearing in states across the country.

Cook vs. Jobs

The company under this CEO [chief executive officer] is an entirely different, and I would say better, animal than it was under Steve Jobs.

Jobs, although he did donate more than he's often given credit for, had a laser-like focus on his company's products as instruments of change. Everything else—activist stances, sustainability, philanthropy—were distractions from what he needed to accomplish with Apple. He was enormously successful on that front, but why couldn't he do both?

There's a school of environmentalism that believes capitalism itself can't do both, especially when it comes to stopping climate change. That, by nature, it gobbles up resources and

Apple's Commitment to a Green Internet

Apple continues to lead the charge in the race to build a green Internet and has significantly increased its impact as a change agent driving renewable energy in the past year. Apple's public commitment to be an environmentally responsible company and specifically to renewable energy has been significantly elevated since Greenpeace's last report and embraced directly by its CEO [chief executive officer] Tim Cook on several occasions. Evidence of the strength of Apple's ongoing commitment to a renewably powered iCloud was strongly demonstrated in the past year as it underwent dramatic growth in its data center infrastructure in both the US and the EU [European Union]; growth that it matched with an equal increase in renewable electricity. Apple's commitment to a 100% renewable cloud appears to be driving change not only among Apple's utility sector partners, but also among other major data center operators that play a supporting role in the delivery of Apple's online products.

Gary Cook and David Pomerantz,
"Clicking Green: A Guide to Building the Green Internet,"
Greenpeace, May 2015.

externalizes environmental damage. While Apple has made strides, it definitely hasn't washed its hands of the massive environmental impact of personal electronics production. This is particularly a problem considering that most manufacturing is outsourced to companies in Asia, which are still overwhelmingly powered by coal.

But can Cook prove it doesn't have to be this way? After all, this isn't a local food co-op we're talking about. This is

Apple, the corporation rated No. 1 in market capitalization in the world. If any company can change the supply chain, this one can.

And the company isn't doing what we find to be the worst of all corporate responsibility strategies: wreaking environmental havoc while simultaneously donating to nonprofits to fix the problem. It really seems to be improving its environmental footprint and pulling multiple levers to do so. Nothing was more encouraging than when a conservative group slammed the CEO for betraying shareholders with its green initiatives.

Cook will perhaps always be remembered for barking at the questioner: "When we work on making our devices accessible by the blind," he said, "I don't consider the bloody ROI [return on investment]." . . .

He didn't stop there, however, as he looked directly at the NCPPR [National Center for Public Policy Research] representative and said, "If you want me to do things only for ROI reasons, you should get out of this stock."

That sounds serious.

One more thing about Tim Cook's green activism: He's clearly a passionate environmentalist, and we now know he's preparing to give away his fortune away. But so far, he's yet to embark on any massive green philanthropy that we know of. My guess is that we can expect that to change, sooner rather than later.

> *"Unfortunately, Amazon ... has made no effort to power with green energy. And it may be getting even dirtier soon."*

Tech Giants Can Be Environmentally Harmful

David Pomerantz

In the following viewpoint, David Pomerantz argues that big tech companies can sometimes be environmentally irresponsible. As a specific example, Pomerantz points out how Amazon, one of the world's largest tech companies, has fallen short in terms of environmental responsibility. At the same time, however, he says that there is much Amazon and other tech companies can do to become more environmentally friendly. Pomerantz is a writer and Greenpeace activist who focuses on topics such as big tech, renewable energy, and Internet electricity demand.

As you read, consider the following questions:

1. According to Pomerantz, how have Apple and Facebook reduced their environmental footprint?

2. Why might Google's decision to open a data center in Ohio be problematic from an environmental perspective, according to the viewpoint?

3. According to Pomerantz, what can Amazon do to make its proposed Ohio data center more environmentally friendly?

"Use the Web? Congrats! You're an environmentalist." So said a headline in the *Washington Post* last week [in November 2014], and with good reason: Some of the biggest names behind the Internet are powering their data centers with wind and solar power.

That's important because the Internet uses a lot of electricity. If the Internet were a country, its electricity demand would rank as the sixth largest in the world.

Tech Giants and the Environment

The *Washington Post* story focused on search engines, and indeed Google, Yahoo, and Microsoft are increasingly powering their data centers with wind power in places like Iowa, Oklahoma, and Texas. But it's not just search: Apple is powering its data centers, replete with all of our iTunes, with 100% renewable energy from wind, solar, geothermal, and microhydro power. Facebook is aiming for the same goal and is purchasing massive quantities of wind power in Iowa to power our likes and shares in its data center there.

One company is sitting out of the race, and it's a crucial one: Amazon.com.

Aside from being one of the most trafficked websites in the world, Amazon also hosts much of the Internet's data via its massive Amazon Web Services (AWS) division, which handles the computing for sites and services like Netflix, Pinterest, Reddit, and Airbnb. According to one 2012 study, one-third of all Internet users visit a website based on Amazon's infrastructure every day.

Unfortunately, Amazon, unlike Google, Apple, Facebook, Yahoo, or Microsoft, has made no effort to power with green energy. And it may be getting even dirtier soon.

Environmental Impact of the Tech Giants

Silicon Valley, California, is recognized globally as the number one address in high technology. It is not only the world's most significant concentration of high-tech industry and talent, but the term "Silicon Valley" itself has become synonymous with a new way of doing business, based upon constant innovation and industrial flexibility.

Unfortunately, the Silicon Valley success story has been blemished by serious environmental degradation. It contains the greatest concentration of "Superfund" National Priorities List sites [hazardous waste sites in the United States eligible for long-term cleanup] in the country. Industrial effluent from high-tech firms has contaminated the San Francisco Bay. Air pollution, principally from motor vehicles, masks the view of the mountain ranges that frame the Santa Clara Valley—the historic name of the region.

Lenny Siegel, "Case Study:
Comparing Apples and Supercomputers:
Evaluating Environmental Risk in Silicon Valley,"
Rockefeller University.

Where Amazon Falls Short

News has been trickling out all fall that Amazon's next data center will be located in Ohio, one of the states in the US that is powered most heavily by coal. So just how much electricity will that facility use?

It's impossible to answer that question precisely, since Amazon is notoriously secretive about its energy use, but we can make a decent estimate. The *Columbus Dispatch* reported last week that Amazon would invest $1.1 billion into the data center. To get from dollars to megawatts, we can make some assumptions and end up with a good estimate that Amazon's Ohio data center would draw about 86 megawatts [MW] of power at full capacity.... Of course, we'd welcome Amazon to provide a more accurate estimate for its new data center's power demand.

Just how much electricity is 86 MW? Well, according to the EPA [Environmental Protection Agency], the average Ohio home draws 895 kWh [kilowatt-hours]/month. So Amazon's new data center will add the same amount of demand to the grid as 70,000 Ohio homes....

That's a lot of juice. If Amazon continues to sit on the sidelines of the green Internet race and just default to use whatever power it gets off the grid, most of that electricity will come from coal-burning power plants. Ohio's electricity mix was powered by 70% coal in 2013. The exact mix being offered in central Ohio by the utility there, American Electric Power [AEP], is less clear, though it's likely in the same range. A 2012 fact book from the company said its Ohio generating capacity was 88.2% powered by coal.

What Amazon Could Do Better

When other IT [information technology] companies have built data centers in areas with similarly dirty electricity grids, they have taken matters into their own hands. In North Carolina, Apple is powering with on-site solar, and it, Google, and Facebook have teamed up to push the utility there, Duke Energy, to offer them more renewable options.

Amazon has options to do as much or more in Ohio. The Ohio State University, located just a few miles from any of the sites Amazon is rumored to be considering, entered a contract last year to buy 50 MW of wind to power much of its campus, saying that it would save $1 million a year in the process. Amazon could ask AEP to provide it with more renewable energy options, or call on Ohio legislators to restore the state's renewable portfolio standard. The Campbell Soup Company modeled that exact kind of positive political advocacy, in addition to building a 10 MW solar farm to power its factory.

So many tech companies are doing the right things to bring us a greener Internet. As a Google spokesperson said in the *Post* story, "Because we've purchased 1,000 megawatts of renewable wind energy for our data centers, you might say using Google is like kite-surfing the Internet."

Unfortunately, using Amazon, or any AWS-hosted site like Netflix or Pinterest, is currently like surfing the Internet on a barge full of coal. A company that has made innovation its hallmark should do better. It can start at its new facility in Ohio.

Periodical and Internet Sources Bibliography

The following articles have been selected to supplement the diverse views presented in this chapter.

Ben Adler	"Which Tech Companies Are the Greenest?," *Mother Jones*, May 14, 2015.
Sebastian Anthony	"Tech Giants Team Up to Battle NSA Surveillance, Governmental Snooping," ExtremeTech, December 9, 2013.
Farhan Attamimi	"The Google Bus: Tech Giants' Social Impact," The Vanguard, May 4, 2014.
Susie Cagle	"The Dark Side of Startup City," *Grist*, July 26, 2013.
Josh Constine	"Google Sets Example by Trying to Offset Perils of SF Gentrification," TechCrunch, February 28, 2014.
Joe Kloc	"Tech Boom Forces a Ruthless Gentrification in San Francisco," *Newsweek*, April 15, 2014.
Mary Mazzoni	"What Does Corporate Responsibility Mean When It Comes to NSA Data Requests?," TriplePundit, July 31, 2014.
Claire Cain Miller	"Angry over U.S. Surveillance, Tech Giants Bolster Defenses," *New York Times*, October 31, 2013.
George Packer	"Change the World," *New Yorker*, May 27, 2013.
Jeff Stone	"Microsoft Becomes Latest Tech Firm to Put Social Issues on the Front Burner," *International Business Times*, March 28, 2015.
Kaveh Waddell	"How Tech Giants Became a Leading Civil-Rights Voice," *National Journal*, April 1, 2015.

OPPOSING
VIEWPOINTS®
SERIES

CHAPTER 2

What Issues Surround the Products of Tech Giants?

Chapter Preface

Today's technology giants offer an incredibly diverse array of products and services that keep customers coming back for each new release. While many of these products and services are obviously well liked and sought after by consumers, some face stiffer criticism. Some ideas that look good on paper can have real-world implications that lead to controversy. Concerns over these more controversial products and services can easily become public relations nightmares for tech companies and can have a serious impact on their bottom lines.

The problems that tech giants encounter with some of their more controversial products and services can be many and varied. In recent years, many tech companies, for example, have been introducing cloud computing services. Although such services can be very useful for private and business consumers alike, questions about the safety and security of cloud servers have led many to doubt whether such technology can be used reliably. In some cases, the criticism is directed at specific tech brands as a whole, as is the case for Apple, which detractors often say charges exorbitantly high prices for its products. In others, criticism focuses on the way tech companies do business. One example of this is the backlash that has come in the wake of Amazon's announcement that it is exploring the possibility of using drones to deliver packages.

Among the most notable instances of a tech giant coming under fire for one of its products is the controversy surrounding Google's experimental Google Glass device. First unveiled in 2013, Google Glass was a wearable smart device that resembled a pair of eyeglasses. Designed to offer wearers a largely hands-free smartphone-like experience with an advanced optical display, Google Glass seemed poised to be an innovation that would transform the tech world. At first, it looked like that might just be the case. Technophiles lauded Google's efforts and praised Google Glass as an important breakthrough. Before long, however, issues with some of the device's capabilities led to an extreme backlash. The strongest and most heated criticism focused on Google Glass's built-in camera, which detractors argued could easily be used to surreptitiously record people without their permission or knowledge. As a result, critics alleged that Google Glass posed an unacceptable threat to personal privacy. Eventually, the public outcry escalated to the point that Google had no choice but to cancel its original plans for the full release of Google Glass and take its pet project back to the laboratory for further refinement.

Google isn't the only tech giant to have encountered criticism over privacy issues. Tech hardware manufacturer Samsung, for example, came under fire in 2015 after it was learned that the built-in microphone used to enable voice commands on Samsung smart TVs was capable of recording any spoken words it picked up and transmitting that data to unidentified third parties. Critics quickly pointed out that if smart TV users verbally revealed personal information in range of their televisions, that sensitive data could potentially end up in the hands of unknown third parties. Similarly, Facebook also came under fire from privacy advocates when it announced that it was working on a facial recognition algorithm that could identify people in photos, even if they were not looking at the camera.

Clearly, tech giants are not immune to failure. The way their products and services are perceived and consumed by the general public determines not only their financial standing but also their creative direction over time. As a result, it is essential for tech companies to carefully monitor and respond to the public outcries concerning their products and services.

Issues that surround the products of tech giants are examined in the following chapter, which explores concerns over

Google Glass, cloud computing services, the price of tech products, and the possibility of delivery drones used by commercial enterprises.

> *"Google Glass has the capability to push our lives into reality of the television kind. But many of us aren't ready for our close-up, and never will be."*

Google Glass Technologies Present Serious Privacy Concerns

Brian Proffitt

In the following viewpoint, Brian Proffitt argues that Google Glass poses some serious privacy concerns that must be addressed before the technology is made widely available. He contends that Google Glass's video-recording capabilities have the potential to violate the privacy of those who are recorded without their permission. He worries that this kind of illicit recording would be not only morally reprehensible but also potentially dangerous. Proffitt is a journalist and author who specializes in technology issues.

As you read, consider the following questions:

1. According to Proffitt, why is being recorded by Google Glass different than being recorded by security cameras?

2. What are some of the ways Proffitt says Google Glass could be abused?

3. According to Mark Hurst, how might Google use the data it collects through Google Glass devices?

Even as many in the geek-o-sphere drool in anticipation for the onset of Google Glass, some technologists are starting to question the very real privacy issues entangled with the use of these wearable computers and cameras.

Predictably, the first concerns raised about Google Glass were about the *user's* privacy: If I am transmitting all of this data to Google, it is going to know even more about me than ever! Or so the reasoning goes. I have to admit that this has been bugging me, but since I carry around an Android phone already, I'm pretty sure Google pretty much knows whatever it wants to know about me.

But then there's the other half of the privacy problem, which not many in the community have yet voiced: What about the privacy of the people these devices are looking *at?*

Anonymous Cameras Everywhere

Being monitored by video cameras is nothing new, of course; it's a risk we run every day. If I happen to absent-mindedly pick my nose in the seemingly empty frozen food aisle at Mega Mart, it's a pretty sure bet that my gross-out was captured on a video somewhere.

The advent of Google Glass supercharges the equation, because now the number of cameras increases—perhaps exponentially—and they'll show up in ever more unexpected places owned by a much wider variety of people and organizations.

For now, there's an implied trust that someone from the store won't take that nose-picking video and put it on You-Tube as part of a "Disgusting Things Journalists Do" montage. Sure, there's nothing really stopping some bored Mega Mart employee from scraping that video for whatever purpose. But,

What Privacy Means

For Google, "privacy" means "what you've agreed to," and that is slightly different from the privacy we've become used to over time. So how comfortable—or uneasy—should we feel about the possibility that what we're doing in a public or semi-public place (or even somewhere private) might get slurped up and assimilated by Google? You can guess what would happen the first time you put on [Google] Glass: There would be a huge scroll of legal boilerplate with "Agree" at the end. And, impatient and uncaring as ever, you would click on it with little regard for what you were getting yourself, and others, into.

Charles Arthur, "Google Glass:
Is It a Threat to Our Privacy?," Guardian, *March 6, 2013.*

should they happen to post said video and I happen to see it, I will likely recognize my surroundings in the video and find someone to sue.

Now imagine the same situation, recorded not by the store's cameras, but by someone wearing a Google Glass or similar device who happened to be standing unnoticed at the end of the aisle. Our voyeur records the incident, posts it on the web anonymously, and—*boom!*—my reasonable expectation of privacy is violated. And I will likely never be able to find the culprit to take the video down.

The lesson here—beyond "don't pick your nose"—is that if these devices do indeed take off, there is nothing to stop someone from monitoring and tagging me in photos, micro-blogs or videos—whether or not I know what's going on.

There can be some positives out of this kind of citizen "Eye in the Sky." If someone commits a crime, for instance, they might have been surreptitiously recorded in the act, with less obvious danger to the recorder than holding up a smart-phone. Indeed, in his novel *Earth*, futurist David Brin outlines a near-future where citizens keep down random street crime just by the existence of video-recording equipment they wear.

But there's a flip side to this, when a collection of Brin's characters, a group of street punks, is befriended by an elderly man who seems to want to teach them about the Way Things Were. It all goes well, until after the senior man's death, the gang discovers to their mortification that the man has been logging every conversation for use in a social-observation article about the state of youth in that society.

A little out there? Maybe so, but how long before Tumblr, Flickr and YouTube are filled with text and video content of embarrassing moments captured by Google Glass?

Anyone Can Be a Target

Beyond the voyeur problem, I keep coming back to how this technology can be abused—particularly this very scary scenario:

Imagine someone builds an app that lets you upload a photo of someone to your Google account and then uses facial-recognition software to process the face of every person you see. Sure, there are benign uses for such a tool, such as helping people remember the names of the people they meet.

But what if I was a member of an (alleged!) criminal organization who would love nothing better than to . . . talk . . . to the witness that's going to testify in the trial that might prove my organization has done some pretty bad things. We're innocent, of course, but it would be nice to . . . explain things . . . to this witness, who is currently ensconced in the U.S. Marshal's Witness Protection Program.

To find that witness today, I'd have to be incredibly lucky, hack the Marshal's computer system or bribe (or threaten?) a corrupt law enforcement official. But in a Google Glass world, I could hire private detectives to be on the lookout for my target. Better yet, I could post an ad on Craigslist offering a reward to find "my long-lost cousin/uncle/aunt." Now I have an entire community of people using facial-recognition software helping me find this person. Heck, you might not have to actively employ Google Glass users. Just periodically run a Google Images search of your target's photo for "Images like this."

Now imagine you're the *witness* in this scenario.

There are lots of times people don't want to be found—spouses seeking to escape an abusive partner, victims trying to elude stalkers—any one of these types of people could run afoul of these cameras. The technology to do this kind of illicit activity is not quite ready for commercial shelves yet, but the day is soon coming.

But the implications are already disturbing: Besides embarrassing videos taken in public, you can add tracking by jealous spouses, overprotective parents or insurance companies to the list. If you're really paranoid, think about government surveillance of legitimate but unpopular activities.

Is this all too much? Maybe. But think about this, because as a father, I sure do: With Google Glass, what's to stop anyone from recording images and audio of children? As a parent, the thought of anyone tracking minors for any reason without parents' permission . . . is abhorrent and potentially dangerous.

The technology itself makes this kind of subtle, continuous recording more likely. Unlike cell phone cameras, Google Glass is always on, always recording, capturing even the quick stuff you can't anticipate. The upshot? Far fewer safe refuges where you're not going to be recorded.

Ready for Your Close-Up?

Plenty of others are worried about how Google Glass will destroy the expectation of privacy in our normal, not-made-for-TV daily lives. Mark Hurst at Creative Good writes (*emphasis his*):

"Google Glass is like one [Street View] camera car for each of the thousands, possibly millions, of people who will wear the device—every single day, everywhere they go—on sidewalks, into restaurants, up elevators, around your office, into your home. From now on, starting today, anywhere you go within range of a Google Glass device, everything you do could be recorded and uploaded to Google's cloud, and stored there for the rest of your life. You won't know if you're being recorded or not; and even if you do, you'll have no way to stop it."

"And that, my friends, is the experience that Google Glass creates. That is the experience, we should be thinking about. The most important Google Glass experience is not the user experience—it's the experience of everyone else. The experience of being a citizen, in public, is about to change."

Whether we are just running errands, hanging out with friends or are on the lam from some really bad people, Google Glass has the capability to push our lives into reality of the television kind. But many of us aren't ready for our close-up and never will be.

> *"The reality is, on one hand, that [Google] Glass does have a number of safeguards built in and there are several ways in which it's easier for you to be recorded by someone with other devices (digital cameras, smartphones) than by someone wearing Glass."*

Google Glass Privacy Concerns Are Overstated

Matt McGee

In the following viewpoint, Matt McGee argues that Google Glass critics are overestimating the privacy concerns related to the technology. He contends that these critics are misrepresenting how Google Glass works and using hysterics to frighten the public and elicit concern over imagined privacy issues. He asserts that Google Glass will not violate personal privacy because people will be able to tell when the device is recording and because people do not have as great a right to privacy in public as they tend to think they do. McGee is the editor in chief of Search Engine Land, *an online magazine focused on the search engine industry.*

As you read, consider the following questions:

1. According to McGee, what is the fundamental problem with the typical criticism of Google Glass?

2. Why would it be difficult for a Google Glass user to secretly record others, according to the viewpoint?

3. According to McGee, how do the current US privacy laws make it legally impossible for Google Glass users to violate others' privacy?

To hear some people tell it, Google Glass is leading us down a path toward a world where every citizen is a walking, hidden spy, surreptitiously recording videos and photos of everything—and everyone—we see. What's more, they're afraid that those videos and images are being posted on the Internet for all the world to see, warts and all.

Some are afraid that Glass is auto-recording (or will) everything it can see or hear, and each word you've ever spoken within earshot of Glass will be available in Google's search index.

These fears typically come from people that don't know how Glass works. They've never worn it. And despite that lack of firsthand knowledge, they've decided that Glass is a privacy disaster waiting to happen.

The problem: Those folks aren't contributing anything of substance to a discussion that needs to take place. Hysterical fearmongering makes for good headlines, but it doesn't advance the conversation.

In this latest installment of our Google Glass Diary series, I'd like to make the case that some of the privacy concerns with Google Glass are overblown, while others are very legitimate issues that we should be discussing. I'm not arguing against any discussion on Glass and privacy; I'm arguing for a more balanced and intelligent discussion than I've seen so far.

What They're Saying About Google Glass and Privacy

A group of US Congress members sent Google a letter in mid-May [2013] with several privacy-related questions about Glass. Among other things, they asked:

- if Glass unintentionally collects data ... ;

- if non-users are also covered by Google's privacy policies and protections;

- if Google Glass will support facial-recognition technology; and

- if Glass stores user data and, if so, how is it protected.

Canadian privacy officials followed suit in mid-June with their own letter to Google on Glass and privacy. Among other things, they asked:

- how Glass complies with data protection laws;

- what data is collected via Glass and is that data shared with developers;

- is Google doing anything about the "surreptitious collection of information about other individuals"; and

- how does Google plan to deal with facial recognition issues in the future.

Beyond governmental questions, some businesses have banned Glass from their premises over privacy concerns. Numerous articles in recent months have covered how strip clubs, casinos, movie theaters and at least a couple restaurants/cafés are putting up proverbial "no Glass allowed" signs.

Consumer Watchdog, a group that's been hammering Google for years over privacy issues, recently described Glass as "one of the most privacy invasive devices ever" and called on Google to give citizens a way to remove videos or photos taken of them by Glass users without permission from Google's servers.

Even Google reportedly banned Glass from its own shareholders' meeting in June! . . . Word spread like wildfire—and plenty of laughter did, too. Reality check: All recording devices were banned.

In a recent UK [United Kingdom] survey, 20 percent of consumers said they think Glass should be banned completely due to privacy issues.

Clearly, there's a lot of concern about Glass and privacy. Some of it is legitimate. Some of it is born of ignorance about how Glass works. And some of it sounds like nothing more than overstated hysterics.

Why Some Privacy Concerns Are Overstated

In its current form, the way Glass is built and the way it works makes some of the public fears over Glass little more than hype. Many of those fears center on the idea that Glass wearers will be secretly taking photos and recording videos of others. But consider this:

- Glass goes into standby mode very quickly. And from there, *it requires noticeable movement/gestures to be activated.* You either have to reach up and touch Glass to activate it, or you have to tilt your head back (like "Randall Meeks" did in the hysterical *Saturday Night Live* skit that wasn't too far from reality).

- When Glass is activated, the user can only photograph what s/he's looking at. There's no quiet way to take pictures around corners or over walls like you could easily do with smartphones and small cameras.

- The camera isn't very powerful and has no zoom capabilities. When I'm taking pictures or shooting video, it's hard to see people (and what they're doing) unless they're within 30–40 feet. A still photographer with a DSLR [digital single-lens reflex] camera that connects to the Internet is much more capable of violating someone's privacy than I am when wearing Glass.

- Photos and videos done with Glass aren't uploaded publicly to the web, despite what some would have you believe. They *are* uploaded privately to Google+ via auto backup and can be shared publicly from there. "Potential privacy violation!" some scream. But that's exactly how iPhone photos work with Apple's Photo Stream app. (However, unlike Photo Stream, you can't currently turn off the auto backup feature on Glass. Google says that's because Glass has limited storage space—16GB, minus space for application information and software libraries—and it doesn't want Glass users to lose their photos and videos or run out of space. I think Google should give users the option of turning off auto backup for Glass, just like they can do when using iOS or Android devices.)

In a group of people, it's almost impossible to activate Glass and take photos/videos without being noticed. Many of the concerns and scenarios that people are dreaming up about Glass could be applied just as equally to smartphones. Consider this:

I walk up to you at our SMX East marketing conference with Glass on and join a conversation that you're having. You might be worried that I'm recording video without your knowledge. There's no red indicator light flashing, after all.

Fair enough. But if I'm shooting video, you *will* see the Glass display cube lit up, and that's a signal I might be recording video. Or I might not.

But what if I walked up to you and joined that conversation without Glass on, but instead with my iPhone tucked into my shirt pocket. . . .

Just like Glass, there's no flashing red light there to let you know that I'm shooting video. I could record the whole conversation and you'd never know. With the smartphone's superior battery life, I could record a lot longer than with Glass. And with its superior audio and video quality, it'd be a much better video than with Glass.

Or forget about the phone-in-pocket scenario. I could be holding my iPhone in my hand, down at waist level, and still be recording the whole conversation without your knowledge.

But you don't hear anyone talking about the privacy dangers of smartphones that can shoot photos and video. Consumer watchdog groups aren't calling for Apple and Samsung and other phone manufacturers to give citizens a way to remove photos that are taken of them with iPhones and other smartphones. You don't see 20 percent of UK citizens saying smartphones should be banned. There's plenty of privacy fear surrounding Glass, but smartphones are capable of the same things (and more) that are driving the fear.

(Despite the above, I do think that Google should add a small red light indicator that flashes when Glass is recording video, primarily to calm people's nerves.)

Google's Response on Glass Privacy

Google addressed Glass and privacy with a few brief comments during its I/O conference in May—when news of that congressional letter broke.

It explained more in the four-page response to that congressional privacy letter. Susan Molinari, Google's VP [vice president] for public policy and government relations, talked about the social cues that make it evident when Glass is in use.

Those social cues are laid out most clearly in a new Google Glass FAQ that the company has just published.

Q: What have you done to inform non-Glass users if a picture or video is being taken?

A: We have built explicit signals in Glass to make others aware of what's happening. First, the device's screen is illuminated whenever it's in use, and that applies to taking a picture or recording a video. Second, Glass requires the user to either speak a command—"OK Glass, take a picture" or "OK Glass, record a video"—or to take an explicit action by pressing the button on the top of Glass's frame. In each case the illuminated screen, voice command or gesture all make it clear to those around the device what the user is doing.

That FAQ contains the most comprehensive look at Glass and privacy—from Google's point of view and in Google's words—that I've seen to date. It's a welcome addition to the privacy discussion, but I suspect Google will need to do much more about educating the public on the subject of Glass and privacy.

Privacy Has to Be Discussed

Don't get me wrong: I'm not saying Glass is free from privacy issues and that no one should worry about or discuss Glass this way. Quite the contrary. There should be—has to be—a discussion about Google Glass and privacy. But it needs less hype, less fear, and more balanced, rational conversation. A few things that conversation should include [the following]:

Facial Recognition. This is one of the hot-button topics with Glass and privacy. There are fears that Glass could allow wearers to learn information about anyone that its camera sees.

Google has already announced that it won't approve any Glass apps that use facial recognition, and the new FAQ says Google isn't planning to add the technology to Glass itself.

Glass doesn't do facial recognition, and we have no plans to add it. Prior to that statement in the Glass FAQ, Google's policy has been that it "won't add facial-recognition features to our products without having strong privacy protections in place." That obviously opens the door to someday allow facial recognition in Glass (and other Google products). So, this is something that needs to continue to be discussed.

Glass and User Data. The new FAQ addresses this topic in a couple different spots. It says that Google doesn't always know what the Glass user is doing or seeing; it points to the company's privacy policy when answering a question about what user data is collected; and it explains that apps specifically indicate what account permissions they need when being installed.

Not mentioned is this little-known fact: Searches that you do via Google Glass don't show up in your Google account's search history. As long as that's the case, you could argue that Google stores less user data from Glass than it does from other devices and platforms.

Still, given Google's history with user data and privacy (think back to the WiSpy and Google Buzz screwups, for example), this is a topic that needs to be discussed more as Glass and its app ecosystem develop.

Glass for Prescription Glasses. Yikes. This is going to get dicey. In that Glass FAQ, Google says it expects to release frames that will let users add prescription lenses to Google Glass.

Great news for glass (lowercase "g") wearers! But just watch the privacy battles roll in left and right.

Casinos, for example, are starting to ban Google Glass, just like they also ban the use of smartphones while gambling. But if Joe Gambler is wearing Google Glass with his prescription lenses, will they tell him he has to gamble with less than full vision? Movie theaters are also starting to say "no Glass" just like they ban talking on phones and recording with smartphone cameras. Are they going to tell Sally Moviefan that she has to take her prescription Google Glass off if she wants to (try to) watch *Iron Man 4*?

Telling consumers they're not allowed to wear prescription glasses because Google Glass is attached sounds like a recipe for trouble.

Current Privacy Laws. In the US, we have laws that give citizens a "reasonable expectation of privacy" and protect them from privacy invasions when such an expectation exists. I'm not a lawyer, but as I understand it, that expectation doesn't exist when you're out shopping, at a sporting event or concert, or pretty much anywhere in public. Others have the right to record you—whether it's with Glass or with any other device. (In Hawaii a couple weeks ago, I was perfectly within my rights to shoot a photo of a stranger sitting on a beach admiring the sunset.)

We'd all be well served to remember this when we're discussing Glass and privacy. If you're out in public, the law already states that you shouldn't expect privacy.

Final Thoughts

Glass isn't the first piece of wearable computing. But it is the most mainstream, and that means we're getting into new territory where personal tech is concerned. Glass already raises many new questions on privacy, and as time passes, there's no doubt it'll raise more—likely some questions that we can't even imagine right now.

But that doesn't justify the hysterics and hype about outlandish scenarios where Glass turns us all into walking spies, secretly recording every movement we make, and every movement the people around us make.

The reality is, on one hand, that Glass does have a number of safeguards built in and there are several ways in which it's easier for you to be recorded by someone with other devices (digital cameras, smartphones) than by someone wearing Glass. On the other hand, there are legitimate privacy issues that we need to work through as more people begin to wear Glass.

As I said, I'm not dismissing *all* of the privacy concerns that Google Glass raises. I'm not dismissing the privacy debate at all. It's a discussion that needs to happen. When it does, let's make sure it's based on real information and awareness, not on fear and hype.

| "For all the benefits of the cloud, it creates new weaknesses in a company's security infrastructure."

Cloud Computing Services Have Inherent Security Risks

Ted Samson

In the following viewpoint, Ted Samson argues that cloud computing services are much less secure than we tend to believe. Citing several key examples of how easily hackers can breach cloud security, he contends that many tech companies are doing a subpar job of protecting users' personal data and that if cloud computing is to be a truly reliable technology, security measures will have to be improved. Samson is a staff writer for InfoWorld.

As you read, consider the following questions:

1. According to the viewpoint, what happened to Mat Honan when his iCloud account was hacked?

2. According to Steve Wozniak, what is the primary problem with cloud computing?

3. According to Samson, why is user data particularly vulnerable in the cloud?

This past weekend [in August 2012], Apple cofounder Steve Wozniak predicted that cloud computing would yield "horrible problems" in coming years. By extraordinary coincidence, *Wired* reporter Mat Honan experienced firsthand a series of horrible, cloud-related problems, all of which reportedly started when an unnamed Apple employee reset his iCloud password at the request of a hacker posing as Honan.

The Weakness of the Cloud

This marks the second high-profile cloud-related snafu in the past week, the first being the Dropbox fiasco where hackers pulled a list of Dropbox customer email addresses from a Dropbox employee's Dropbox account. The incidents almost render moot the raging debate over on Sophos' *Naked Security* blog as to whether Microsoft's newly rebooted Outlook.com should support more than a 16-character limit on passwords. Evidently even the strongest, most complex password is no match for the formidable combination of hacker perseverance and resourcefulness and end user naiveté (or ignorance) about best security practices.

Let's start with what happened to *Wired*'s Honan. By his account, a malicious hacker gained entry to his iCloud account and used it to remote wipe all of his devices, including his iPhone, iPad, and MacBook Air. The initial mystery: How did the hacker get his or her hands on Honan's password? "My password was a 7-digit alphanumeric that I didn't use elsewhere. When I set it up, years and years ago, that seemed pretty secure at the time," Honan wrote.

Honan's first guess was that hacker employed brute force techniques to crack the password. While that might have been feasible, it wasn't the case. "They got in via Apple tech support and some clever social engineering that let them bypass security questions," Honan wrote in an update.

Once the hacker got into Honan's iCloud account, it was a matter of time before he or she was able to wipe Honan's iDe-

A Cloud with No Silver Lining

If it's in the cloud—a public, free cloud service, especially—then chances are good that eventually it will find its way to the Internet. Cloud services are leaky by their nature; things that are supposed to be private get stored alongside things that are shared, and anything from user error to a previously undiscovered vulnerability can make even strong passwords pointless, while exposing all of those things to the world.

Sean Gallagher, "Update:
What Jennifer Lawrence Can Teach You About Cloud Security,"
Ars Technica, September 1, 2014.

vices, as well as wreaking other havoc, such as changing his Gmail account password and purging that account.

A Serious Concern

Was this the kind of nightmare Wozniak was contemplating this past weekend when he told an audience that he "really worries about everything going into the cloud"?

"I think it's going to be horrendous. I think there are going to be a lot of horrible problems in the next five years," Wozniak said, according to AFP [Agence France-Presse]. "With the cloud, you don't own anything. You already signed it away," he added, along with, "The more we transfer everything onto the Web, onto the cloud, the less we're going to have control over it."

It's entirely plausible Wozniak was thinking in broader terms about data ownership and the prospect of cloud providers treating customer data and files as their own. For example, an unethical company might hide terms in cloud contracts that permit it to mine customer data in the name of research or for more nefarious purposes. A cloud company might also try to shackle customers in how they can use, say, e-books, videos, or software they legally bought and paid for. Heck, a cloud company could go rogue and hold a customer's data hostage or sell it to the highest bidder.

Those are potential threats pertaining to how much control one has over his or her cloud-stored data, but they aren't the only issues. Part of the threat lies in just how interconnected data and devices and identities become in the cloud, all of which can become breached by bypassing a single password.

Consider for a moment the fact that, thanks to one gullible Apple employee giving up a customer's iCloud password, said customer lost all the contents of his cloud-connected devices (hopefully not permanently). Consider that thanks to an ignorant Dropbox employee's actions of reusing passwords and storing sensitive, unencrypted customer info in the cloud, a bunch of Dropbox customers became victims of massive spam attacks, which easily could have been more dangerous phishing attacks.

For all the benefits of the cloud, it creates new weaknesses in a company's security infrastructure. Both Dropbox and Apple have failed at embracing and enforcing necessary security measures to protect users. Cloud users, both customers and employees, meanwhile, continue to ignore or underestimate cloud-related risks. Yes, we can rail at the Apple employee for letting a hacker bypass Honan's security questions, but then, a resourceful hacker could potentially dig up the correct answers to security questions through some research on Facebook, targeted phishing, and the like.

"*Leading enterprise cloud computing and data storage service providers . . . employ the best and brightest IT security experts and devote significant portions of their huge budgets to ensuring they are using the latest threat monitoring and cloud security solutions available.*"

Cloud Computing Services Are Safe and Likely to Get Safer

Andrew Burger

In the following viewpoint, Andrew Burger argues that while there is an ever growing host of security threats facing cloud computing services today, most clouds are safer and more secure than critics claim. He contends that major tech companies such as Google and Microsoft take cloud security threats seriously and are doing everything they can to ensure that their cloud servers—and users' data by extension—are as safe from hackers and other threats as possible. Burger is a journalist who specializes in technology, ecology, sociology, and political economy.

As you read, consider the following questions:

1. According to Burger, who is most responsible for ensuring cloud security?

2. What is currently the best method for securing cloud computing systems, according to the viewpoint?

3. According to RightScale, why is cloud security becoming less of a concern?

Businesses large and small are turning to cloud computing systems to forge leaner, more effective and efficient organizations. Amid explosive growth in the use of Internet-connected devices, deployments of the latest in mobile broadband infrastructure and the fast emerging "Internet of Things (IoT)," cloud computing is becoming the core of a new generation of information systems (IS) architecture.

Besides opening up a world of "Big Data" and "Always-On Connectivity," the exponential increase in the number of "things" with IP [Internet protocol] addresses opens up vast opportunities for those looking to exploit security weaknesses in connected devices, networks and servers. That includes alleged government cyber-espionage campaigns as well as an ever growing variety of increasingly sophisticated cyber-attacks on the part of cyber-criminals and terrorists.

As the OpenSSL Heartbleed vulnerability and Dragonfly malware group have demonstrated, these malware and cyber-threats now have the capability to exploit vulnerabilities in encryption methods and technology, and access network, server and application software to control industrial processes. They can even control critical public infrastructure, such as power, energy and water distribution systems.

Recent malware invasions and security breaches notwithstanding, the cloud computing migration appears unstoppable. According to RightScale's "2014 State of the Cloud Survey," public cloud adoption among 1,068 organizations surveyed is nearing 90 percent. That begs the question: Are the organizations contemplating a shift to cloud IS architectures concerned about security risk? More fundamentally: Just how secure is cloud data storage?

The Growing Cloud

Global shipments of smart-connected devices, including everything from PCs [personal computers] to wearable electronics and household appliances, surpassed 1 billion in 2013 and are expected to approach 1.8 billion this year, according to a forecast from IDC [International Data Corporation].

As these devices become a part of everyday life, they span the divide between work and home, creating problems for corporate IT security departments. The BYOD, "Bring Your Own Device," and BYOA, "Bring Your Own Application," trends put further pressure on IT security departments and spur another step-change in the evolution and growing use of cloud computing services.

From data storage and software as a service (SaaS), the diversity of cloud computing services has expanded to include broader IT outsourcing options—so-called platform as a service (PaaS) and infrastructure as a service (IaaS).

According to RightScale's 2014 cloud technology survey, cloud computing is approaching ubiquity, with uptake fastest among enterprise-scale organizations:

- 94 percent of organizations surveyed are running applications or experimenting with infrastructure as a service;

- 87 percent of organizations are using public cloud;

- 74 percent of enterprises have a hybrid cloud strategy and more than half of those are already using both public and private cloud.

Then there are consumers, who are increasingly making use of cloud services, such as Amazon Cloud Drive, Apple iCloud, Google Drive and Microsoft's SkyDrive, as well as a growing host of niche cloud services providers, such as Dropbox, SugarSync and Box, to store and access digital content from mobile, desktop, small office and home consumer electronic (CE) devices and systems.

Securing the Cloud

Securing all of those electronic devices, networks, proprietary data and information from incursions by cyber-spies and criminals is of paramount concern to organizations of all stripes, and it is straining the capacity of the IT [information technology] resources of even the largest and most experienced. That's particularly true when it comes to those new to cloud computing or in the early stages of contemplating cloud deployment.

Besides individual end users, organizations and cloud computing services vendors, the onus of assuring the security of the cloud falls squarely on the shoulders of IT security software and systems vendors such as Symantec.

Highlighting the seriousness of cloud security threats, Symantec recently reported on an ongoing, sophisticated, very possibly state-sponsored "cyber espionage campaign dubbed Dragonfly (aka Energetic Bear)" that managed to infiltrate information systems of "energy grid operators, major electricity generation firms, petroleum pipeline operators and energy industry industrial control system (ICS) equipment manufacturers" around the world.

Data security and protection, as well as assuring personal privacy, is inherently an issue of corporate social responsibility (CSR). As Cecily Joseph, Symantec vice president of corporate responsibility, told 3p [TriplePundit]: "At Symantec, we enable people and businesses to enjoy the connected world by protecting their most important assets—their memories and data.

"Symantec considers the protection of information— whether it's in the cloud, on your mobile or desktop—central to the responsibility of corporations in this digital age. Our customers trust us with the data they capture, share and save online. Trust is at the heart of the relationships we cultivate, and the responsibility we have to our customers, partners and communities."

One of the ways Symantec aims to assuage enterprises' cloud security concerns is a platform dubbed O$_3$ "that provides single sign-on and enforces access control policies across web applications." As the company explains, "O$_3$ helps enterprises migrate to software as a service (SaaS) applications while ensuring that proper risk management and compliance measures are in place to protect enterprise data and follow regulations."

More broadly, the Open Data Center Alliance (ODCA), surveying the likes of Deutsche Telekom, Disney and SAP regarding enterprise cloud computing and services, found that 66 percent of organizations are concerned about cloud security. Its market research with leading enterprises also led ODCA to produce a suite of new enterprise white papers on cloud computing requirements and best practices, including "the first available enterprise IT perspective on security and privacy."

Public, Private, and Hybrid Clouds

Proponents contend that making use of public cloud services and data storage solutions from leading providers enhances data and IS security. They point out that leading enterprise cloud computing and data storage service providers such as Amazon Web Services, Google, Microsoft, OpenStack and IT virtualization specialist VMWare employ the best and brightest IT security experts and devote significant portions of their huge budgets to ensuring they are using the latest threat monitoring and cloud security solutions available.

Others beg to disagree. As cloud security start-up Jump-Cloud cofounder Rajat Bhargava said in a recent interview:

"There's no more debate. When you don't own the network, it's open to the rest of the world, and you don't control the layers of the stack, the cloud—by definition—is more insecure than storing data on premises."

The Cloud and the Internet of Things

Adding impetus to the cloud computing migration is the desire to latch on to, and capitalize on, the fast emerging "Internet of Things" (IoT). Surveying 400 IT professionals in the U.S. and U.K. on behalf of network control systems developer Infoblox, Coleman Parkes Research Ltd. found that 90 percent of respondents' enterprises are either planning or already implementing network solutions to manage the huge increase in traffic the IoT is anticipated to bring.

According to Gartner, the installed base of "things" connected to the Internet will grow nearly 30-fold, to 26 billion units, in 2020 from 0.9 billion in 2009. "Things" in this context excludes PCs, tablets and smartphones.

"Network administrators have struggled in recent years to stay on top of the 'bring your own device' (BYOD) trend, and the IoT will create an increase in end points that is an order of magnitude greater," said Cricket Liu, chief infrastructure officer at Infoblox, a provider of network control software and systems.

"At the same time, many network teams will have to respond to the IoT without significant increases in budgets or head count. Network automation will become crucial as IT departments confront this massive growth in network complexity."

Are Cloud Security Threats Overblown?

New security threats are anticipated as IoT deployments expand. Nearly two-thirds (63 percent) of respondents to the Coleman Parkes market research report believe IoT to be a threat to network security. On the other hand, 37 percent believe such concerns are overblown and amount to hype.

Cloud services are still at a stage where they are evolving rapidly, as are cyber-threats. That compounds the challenge and raises the risks associated with the quest to realize new revenue streams and gains in productivity, as well as the greater flexibility and lower IT costs, cloud adoption promises.

Seen as the best means of supplementing IS security methods and tools such as multifactor authentication (MFA), wholesale data encryption is being touted as the best means of assuring the security of data, networks and overall IS, whether it be data stored on public, private or hybrid cloud systems.

Yet, as Heartbleed and Dragonfly demonstrate, even public key infrastructure (PKI) and SSL (Secure Sockets Layer)—the core method and means of data encryption—as well as virtual private networks (VPNs), are vulnerable and under attack. Gartner forecasts that there will be a dramatic rise in the use of SSL in cyber-attacks in coming years, with over half of all network attacks making use of encryption by 2017.

As occurred with previous waves of IT innovation, such as outsourcing of data processing, storage, applications and customer services to third-party providers, IT industry experts contend that greater familiarity with cloud computing and services will assuage end users' concerns. Results from RightScale's 2014 cloud survey bear this out. "While the benefits of the cloud increase with experience, the challenges of cloud show a sharp decrease as organizations gain expertise with cloud," RightScale concludes.

"Security remains the most often cited challenge among Cloud beginners (31 percent) but decreases to the fifth most cited (13 percent) among cloud focused organizations. As organizations become more experienced in cloud security options and best practices, the less of a concern cloud security becomes. Concerns about cloud security declined in 2014 among both cloud beginners and cloud focused respondents."

> *"In just the last year, the market has rapidly shifted. Now, Apple's products appear to be overpriced compared to their rivals, and they aren't necessarily better."*

Tech Products Are Overpriced

Sam Mattera

In the following viewpoint, Sam Mattera argues that some tech products are unreasonably overpriced. In particular, he asserts that Apple products, which were once high quality enough to legitimize their astronomical price tags, are no longer worth the exorbitant extra cost. He adds that many other tech companies are offering comparable products that are just as good and sometimes even better than Apple's at less cost to consumers. Mattera is a technology specialist with the Motley Fool, a multimedia financial services company.

As you read, consider the following questions:

1. According to Mattera, why is Apple's iPhone not doing as well in some foreign markets as other tech companies' phones?

2. Why does Apple attract customers even though its prices are so high, according to the viewpoint?

3. According to Mattera, what important change has Apple undergone in recent years?

Apple's rapid growth in recent years has been the product of an extraordinary value offering: Since their introduction, both the iPhone and iPad have been the best products at the best price points. In the past, consumers looking to buy a smartphone or tablet could go with a competitor's product, but they wouldn't be saving any money—and they'd be getting an inferior device.

But, times have changed.

In just the last year [2013], the market has rapidly shifted. Now, Apple's products appear to be overpriced compared to their rivals, and they aren't necessarily better.

The iPhone Is Getting Undercut Both at Home and Abroad

Ask most Americans what an iPhone costs, and they would probably tell you about $200. That's the price the majority of them pay because major mobile carriers (AT&T, Verizon, Sprint and T-Mobile) cover the rest. But, in emerging markets it's quite different; carrier subsidies are practically unheard of. There, consumers often have to pay the full price of the device up front, and given that consumers in those markets, on average, earn far less money, that can be quite a hurdle.

Apple's new iPhone 5C—the company's cheaper model—will retail for about $733 in China, roughly equivalent to the average monthly salary in the world's most populous country. Is it any wonder, then, that (in China) the iPhone's market share is less than 5%?

Google's Android powers the majority of smartphones in China, where local vendors like Lenovo, Xiaomi, and Huawei offer high-end phones at bargain prices. Xiaomi's Red Rice is, from a technological perspective, about as powerful as the iPhone 5C, but retails for just $130.

Even in the U.S., Apple is being undercut. Although flagship smartphones from major competitors like Samsung, HTC, and Motorola also cost roughly $200 on contract, Google's Nexus 4 retails for just $199 unlocked. That means budget-conscious consumers can either buy a Nexus 4 (a phone that's about as powerful as the iPhone 5C) off-contract and go with a cheaper, prepaid carrier, or stick with a major carrier, but stay off-contract.

The iPad Is Now One of the Most Expensive Tablets on the Market

The Nexus 4, despite offering insane value, remains a fairly low-volume phone. Google doesn't really advertise it, and most Americans appear to be fine with the wireless contract model.

But, the tablet market is far different. Subsidized tablets do exist, but most are still bought off-contract. Thus, consumers (even in rich countries like the U.S.) are far more susceptible to price differences in tablets than they are in phones.

In just the last year, a huge gap has opened between the iPad and its rivals. The full-size iPad retails for $500. In past years, this was a fair price, as other 10-inch tablets were just as costly, if not more so—Motorola's Xoom, the first major Android tablet, went on sale in 2011 for $600.

But, as with phones, times have changed. The iPad's competitors appear to have settled on the $300–400 price range as the fair value for a 10-inch tablet. Microsoft's Surface RT retails for $349, Google's Nexus 10 and Samsung's Galaxy Tab 3 go for $399, and Amazon's Kindle Fire HD is just $269 (though to be fair, its screen is only 8.9 inches).

When it comes to smaller tablets, it's even worse. The iPad Mini is an inch larger than most of its Android rivals, but that extra inch costs a lot. At $329, the iPad Mini is $100 more ex-

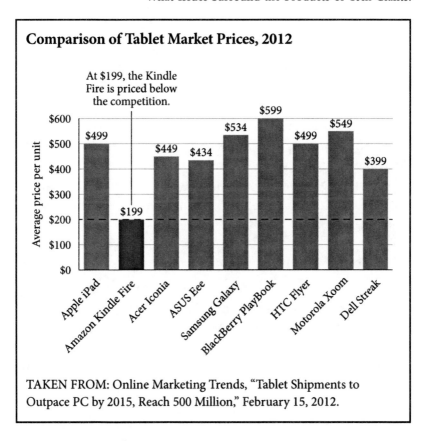

Comparison of Tablet Market Prices, 2012

At $199, the Kindle Fire is priced below the competition.

Average price per unit

Apple iPad — $499
Amazon Kindle Fire — $199
Acer Iconia — $449
ASUS Eee — $434
Samsung Galaxy — $534
BlackBerry PlayBook — $599
HTC Flyer — $499
Motorola Xoom — $549
Dell Streak — $399

TAKEN FROM: Online Marketing Trends, "Tablet Shipments to Outpace PC by 2015, Reach 500 Million," February 15, 2012.

pensive than Google's Nexus 7. It's also significantly less powerful, with a slower processor, lower resolution screen, and worse camera.

How Much Does an Ecosystem Matter?

Despite being overpriced relative to their competition, people continue to buy Apple's products. Apple has a monopoly on one thing its competitors lack: iOS. The mobile operating system continues to be highly regarded, both for its ease of use and its app ecosystem.

Compare that to Microsoft: Despite a heavy ad campaign, including a $1 billion push for Windows 8, sales of its Surface RT tablet have been poor and the company was forced to take a $900 million write-down last quarter.

Based on hardware specs alone, the Surface RT isn't bad. It's about as powerful as the full-size iPad, but also has some key features the iPad lacks, like a USB port and the ability to expand its storage with an SD card. However, because it runs Windows RT, it's fundamentally flawed.

Unlike iTunes, the Windows app store is terrible, missing numerous key apps like LinkedIn, Amazon Video, and HBO Go. Although these services can be accessed through a browser, consumers prefer dedicated apps. Research firm Flurry found that 80% of the time people are using a mobile device, they're using an app.

What Is iOS Worth?

In the past, buying an Apple device was an easy choice. They made the best products and sold them at the best prices. Nowadays, it isn't so clear—Apple might still make the best devices, but they are far from fairly priced. In the end, it really boils down to iOS: its value to consumers and the premium they're willing to pay for it. If iOS is worth that extra $100— and it may be—Apple has nothing to fear.

But, investors should recognize that, over just the last year, things have changed for Apple. It has gone from a value leader to a premium brand, and the long-term ramifications of that shift aren't readily apparent.

> *"No matter how many people say it and how often they do, Apple's products are good enough to justify the prices, even though they are often higher than the competition."*

Tech Products Are Not Overpriced

James Kendrick

In the following viewpoint, James Kendrick explains that it is unfair to label some tech products as overpriced just because they are more expensive than others. Kendrick specifically focuses on Apple products, which have long been branded by critics as overpriced. He contends that Apple's prices are directly reflective of the quality of its products. Because the company offers some of the highest quality tech products, its prices, though high, are justified. Kendrick is a mobile technology expert and a contributing writer for ZDNet.

As you read, consider the following questions:

1. According to Kendrick, what duty do all companies have to their shareholders and customers?

James Kendrick, "Latest Financial Numbers Show Apple's Gadgets Are Not Overpriced," ZDNet, January 29, 2015. www.zdnet.com. Used with permission of ZDNET.com. Copyright © 2015. All rights reserved.

2. Why are Apple's customers willing to pay more for Apple products, according to Kendrick?

3. According to the viewpoint, what proves that Apple's pricing strategy is working?

Apple has posted huge numbers for the previous quarter [fourth quarter 2014], and even so there's no stopping claims that the company is headed for a fall. Many reasons are given, but the old standby is flying around. That's the one that claims Apple's products are overpriced, and that will bring the company to the brink.

This is funny. No matter what you feel about Apple, its products, or its practices, there is no denying the fact that it keeps racking up massive sales. Whether it's the iPad, iPhone, or Macs [personal computers], tens of millions of them keep shipping to customers.

The latest quarter was somewhat of an exception. Those numbers were even higher than anyone expected due to heavy iPhone sales. Of course, that leads some to claim that dependence on high sales of a single product is troubling. Maybe that's true at some level, but in the profit arena not so much.

How Apple Sets Its Prices

To put the "Apple products are overpriced" argument to bed, let's look at what that means. If by overpriced people mean compared to the competition, perhaps they are priced too high. Actually, if a product with a high price sells in high volumes, the competitor's pricing doesn't matter. Or if overpriced means products are too expensive for some to afford them, then in a way they are overpriced. For those customers, anyway.

But in the business world, it's obvious to this writer that Apple is pricing its main products just right. How can that be?

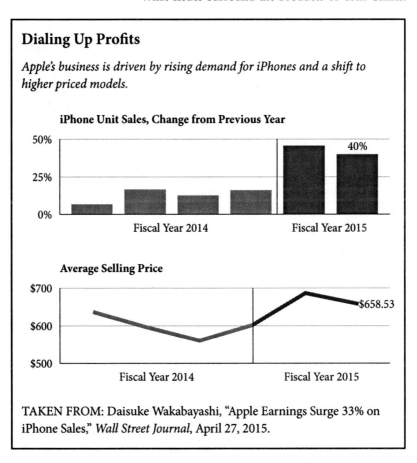

Dialing Up Profits

Apple's business is driven by rising demand for iPhones and a shift to higher priced models.

iPhone Unit Sales, Change from Previous Year

40%

Fiscal Year 2014   Fiscal Year 2015

Average Selling Price

$658.53

Fiscal Year 2014   Fiscal Year 2015

TAKEN FROM: Daisuke Wakabayashi, "Apple Earnings Surge 33% on iPhone Sales," *Wall Street Journal*, April 27, 2015.

Every company has a duty to shareholders and to customers to provide value for every investment. Pivotal to this effort is the proper pricing of products, which involves meeting three criteria:

1. Quality design and build quality that provides sufficient value to customers.

2. Pricing the product at a price a lot of customers are willing to pay.

3. Price point yields the desired profit margin.

That's a simplification, but it's the basis for good pricing practices. The quality criterion is a prerequisite for the second requirement. The easiest way to fulfill the profit criterion is to price products as high as the first two requirements will allow.

When a company meets all three requirements and posts sales in volume, then the pricing is good as gold. If the value is not there for customers, they will not buy the products.

Why Apple's Prices Work

Apple's customers see good value in the products as big sales numbers consistently prove. Take the last quarter alone: Over 74 million iPhone purchasers happily paid the price that others will claim is too high.

That this many consumers were willing to pay Apple's prices for the iPhone proves it was well priced. It also makes a rather strong case that had the prices been lower, then the company would have failed to meet its responsibility to shareholders. Other companies may be happy to leave money on the table, but not Apple.

No matter how many people say it and how often they do, Apple's products are good enough to justify the prices, even though they are often higher than the competition. The perceived value is there at purchase time, and the millions of repeat customers prove it's there through the product life cycle.

The high sales volume over time clearly demonstrates that Apple has this pricing thing nailed down. High enough to generate huge profits, yet low enough to get long lines of customers to buy its products. That's not overpricing, that's right pricing.

You may feel that the iPhone is overpriced, but 74 million others disagree.

> *"Drones have the potential to lower cost [and] environmental impact, depending upon their power sources, traffic congestion on the ground, and delivery time windows."*

Delivery Drones Are a Good Idea

Christa Avampato

In the following viewpoint, Christa Avampato argues in favor of the use of delivery drones. In analyzing Amazon's proposed idea to use drones to deliver items sold on its website directly to customers' doorsteps, Avampato concludes that such drones offer many potential benefits and should be put in service. She supports her conclusion by explaining exactly how drones might be used to improve convenience and efficiency in a variety of applications. Avampato is a writer and product developer based in Washington, DC.

As you read, consider the following questions:

1. According to the viewpoint, how might drone delivery improve the grocery business?

131

2. How might drones be used for humanitarian purposes, according to Avampato?

3. According to Avampato, how could drones be useful to insurance agencies?

The media world is buzzing with the news about Amazon's drone delivery development dubbed Amazon Prime Air. In an interview between Charlie Rose and Amazon CEO [chief executive officer] Jeff Bezos on *60 Minutes*, the world learned that Amazon's goal is to use drones to deliver orders to customers in 30 minutes—faster than pizza delivery! . . .

"It will happen," said Bezos. "Next year is optimistic. Maybe more like five years." Bezos, perhaps one of, if not the, most ambitious and determined business leaders of our day, relentlessly pursues opportunities on the fringes and seems much less concerned about cost than most other CEOs. Amazon invents the market and then does its best to move it, alter it, and adapt as quickly and efficiently as possible. This drone R&D [research and development] news stirs thoughts of the opportunities that consumers and businesses face should the drone delivery mechanism become a viable option.

Groceries

Amazon spent five years perfecting their food delivery system that's akin to FreshDirect, Peapod, and other similar services. This summer [2013] it expanded to Los Angeles from its native Seattle. The window of possible delivery time is three hours long.

Both of my local grocery stores, Whole Foods [Market] and West Side Market, offer to deliver my purchases to my home if I don't feel like carrying them. Their delivery window is two hours, so I rarely utilize it. Milk that's two hours old isn't an appetizing prospect, though Amazon puts those kinds of items in temperature-controlled tote bags that it picks up with the next delivery. My local grocery stores don't offer that option.

With efficient packing, faster turnaround, and more precise scheduling, drones could take the place of the mammoth delivery trucks and make grocery delivery the new norm.

Prepared Food Delivery

In New York City, where I live, prepared food delivery is a way of life for many people. GrubHub and Seamless are lifelines. When I spent the summer in LA, I learned that prepared food delivery is a luxury and a rarity. With drones, the benefit of just-in-time prepared food could become commonplace.

U.S. Mail

The U.S. Postal Service is an iconic symbol of our country, though every year it runs a significant deficit. In 2012, it lost $15.9 billion—$11.1 billion of that went to prepayments on future retiree benefits. This year, the loss amounted to $5 billion. While a significant improvement in total over last year, it didn't have the retiree benefit payments concerns of 2012, and that means it's a slightly higher loss from operations.

Package and mail delivery in all forms could be made cheaper and faster with drones in a time when the federal government could use every extra dollar it can find to work on issues such as education, the environment, and health care. By extension, services like UPS [United Parcel Service] and FedEx could also benefit from drone package delivery.

Humanitarian and Medical Supplies

As much as I love the items I order on Amazon, I rarely need them in 30 minutes. Certainly I want them faster, though it's not a matter of life or death that I get the new Malcolm Gladwell book immediately.

The Future of Drone Technology

Until more of the public sees unmanned aerial vehicles in the public sphere, military drones are still the first thing most people think of in relation to the technology. And some of the concerns raised by that association are legitimate. If the technology isn't reliable and operators can't be held accountable, drones don't have to be killing anyone to be problematic.

However, like any military technology that ends up in recreational and commercial spheres, it will take development to get to a level where people can trust drones to fly over their heads safely. And development is only possible through repeated tests, not by making the technology illegal. . . .

The more we see unmanned aerial vehicles doing everyday things, the less we associate them with warfare. And the more companies are forced to prove their technology is safe and reliable, the more it will open up space for the development of that technology. It may take time to solve the more complicated problem of airspace, and to bring moral reasonability to the technology, but if and when that happens, the sky's the limit.

Sabrina Nemis, "Our Problem with Drones,"
Fulcrum *(University of Ottawa), April 2, 2015.*

For items like medical and emergency supplies, we need technology like drones. Some victims of Hurricane Sandy waited days for supplies. It took a week to get desperately needed items to the Philippines after Typhoon Haiyan. Those affected by drought and famine in the developing world can go months without food, proper drinking water, and medical items.

Of course there are other complications beyond logistics such as politics, customs, and security, though logistics certainly play a part in slowing down the process. Surely if we can eventually get a book to someone in 30 minutes, we should be able to do something to improve the distribution of humanitarian relief.

Insurance Claims Adjustments

Speaking of Hurricane Sandy, it took nearly a year for some victims to have the damage to their property assessed. The holdup? There are just so many FEMA [Federal Emergency Management Agency] claims adjustors to go around.

Outfitted with the right technology, drones could eventually supplement claims adjustment officers. We use them to take pictures in outer space. Some schools of journalism use them now to explore areas deeply affected by environmental events. Drones can take us to places we can't go on our own, and they can get us there much faster with less expense and without sacrificing our personal safety.

Drone Delivery Companies

This technology also presents an interesting entrepreneurial opportunity. Amazon has the wherewithal to build its own drone delivery system. Many companies, perhaps even most, don't have the financial nor technological capability in-house to build this service.

We could see the rise of drone delivery companies and perhaps Amazon [could] white label its own drones for use by others, as it has with Amazon Web Services. Interesting tidbit: With clients like Netflix and the CIA [US Central Intelligence Agency], Amazon Web Services is primed to become the largest profit driver of Amazon in the not-too-distant future. Not bad for a company that started selling books online, delivered to the post office by Jeff Bezos himself.

Personal Drones

Let's face it. We've been in love with the idea of robots doing our bidding for decades. Rosie the Robot of *The Jetsons*, KITT from *Knight Rider*, and the Roomba vacuum hold a certain mystique and fascination. Make our meals, drive us around, and vacuum our homes.

But are we limiting ourselves by only seeing drones as machines that just take orders? Could we eventually send them out of the house on our behalf à la Harry Potter's owl, Hedwig? Can we take them shopping with us as a personal attaché and assistant to carry our packages, give us directions, deliver important reminders, and help us spot deals? Do they become companions in our daily lives while also providing valuable services? Never underestimate a robot.

The Challenges of a Drone Future

Jeff Bezos made more than an announcement about his company's latest technological development. He gave us a glimpse into the future that is not only possible but also probable. Drones have the potential to lower cost [and] environmental impact, depending upon their power sources, traffic congestion on the ground, and delivery time windows while increasing tracking capabilities, precision scheduling, and our ability to get to places that are difficult for us to reach in person.

However, the complications and complexities are many. Bezos himself alluded to the logistical, political, and security minefields that drone technology must cross before it can be implemented and scaled. My next . . . piece will address these challenges in detail.

| "*Amazon drones are a completely ridiculous and unworkable idea, of course, and will (no pun intended) never get off the ground.*"

Delivery Drones Are a Bad Idea

James Brumley

In the following viewpoint, James Brumley argues that Amazon's proposal to use drones to deliver packages is a bad idea that will never work from a practical perspective. He contends that there are far too many obstacles for drone delivery to ever be a realistic possibility. As such, he believes the idea will never actually come to fruition. Brumley is a writer and former stock broker whose work has been published on such websites as Investor-Place, the Motley Fool, and Investopedia.

As you read, consider the following questions:

1. Why does Brumley say it would be difficult to operate delivery drones in urban areas?

2. What would likely happen if a delivery drone experienced an in-flight technical failure, according to the viewpoint?

3. According to Brumley, why is it important that delivery drones be manned?

If the story on Amazon drones hadn't aired on TV's deadpan-serious *60 Minutes*, it would have been easy to assume Sunday's [December 1, 2013] announcement from Amazon.com CEO [chief executive officer] Jeff Bezos was something cooked up by spoof site *The Onion*, or perhaps one of Google's now predictable April Fools' Day news releases.

It wasn't a joke, though.

Drones in Amazon's Future?

In a development that was once something only hypothesized in the cartoon/fantasy world of *The Jetsons*, Bezos says the company is developing airborne Amazon drones to deliver many of the online retailer's goods to its paying customers.

That's right. Amazon feels it's only a matter of time—and not even much of it—before card-table-sized octocopters will be dropping off purchases right at your doorstep. Once the delivery is made, the drone will fly back to its distribution center to pick up and deliver the next payload.

Amazon drones are a completely ridiculous and unworkable idea, of course, and will (no pun intended) never get off the ground anytime in our lifetimes.

Still, it's fun to see someone of Jeff Bezos's ilk have as much faith as he has that science fiction is becoming scientific fact.

The response to the announcement has been what you might expect; half of the public loves the premise, while the other half is proverbially rolling their eyes. What's interesting is that *even the folks who love the idea* don't actually seem to think it's going to be become a reality anytime soon . . . despite Bezos's optimism.

Thing is, their intuition might be spot-on.

Here are the three biggest reasons Amazon drones are going to be grounded before ever taking flight.

1: The coverage areas for Amazon drones are inherently full of airborne hazards.

It wasn't one of the underscored details of the *60 Minutes* interview, but the proposed battery-operated drone that Amazon is working on only has an operating range of about 10 miles from its takeoff point; the service will only be available in fairly metropolitan areas near an Amazon hub.

It's not really a customer service problem, as nobody *expects* the company to lose money just to offer the delivery option in rural areas. Besides, rollouts of all sorts tend to begin in metropolitan areas and work their way outward.

No, the problem with populous areas—where the service makes fiscal sense—is that these areas can be loaded with tall buildings, power lines, cranes, birds and a million other things that could (literally) get in the way. And that's partially why . . .

2: Any in-flight failure will turn into a disaster.

While it would be inaccurate to say in-flight failures are common for these electric octocopters, it wouldn't be inaccurate to say failures *do* happen from time to time. And, unlike failures in airplanes where the plane at least has a shot at being glided to safety, a failure on a couple (or more) of the delivery drones' eight rotors means a five-pound package—in addition to the weight of the drone itself—becomes a rock falling out of the sky.

What happens when—not if—it lands in the middle of a busy road, or worse, lands on a moving car?

It's a remote possibility, but so are lighting strikes, and those kill about 50 people per year. Of course, lightning has the benefit of being an uncontrollable product of nature.

Were there no alternative, it might be a case where the public simply had to suck it up and deal with the risks. However, with a trio of safe, viable delivery-to-door services read-

Who Needs a Delivery Drone?

Drones are inherently noisy, an extreme security risk (bomb delivery with pinpoint accuracy), an invasion of privacy (cameras), they can injure people with their propellers by accident and they can fall out of the sky. . . .

Drones are a serious hazard to civil aviation. Hitting a drone is worse than hitting a bird. Drones have hard metal parts and a dense battery. A drone goes into a jet engine and it's done. A drone goes into the tail rotor of a helicopter and that helicopter is going down.

A fleet of delivery drones is also the "hive of bees" air defense/offense; and since they are controlled by software they could be hacked to attack aviation with relative ease. The "hive" of drones can take down any aircraft (military or civilian) in the sky just by positioning themselves so nothing can get past them. There is nothing we have today, military or civilian, that can defeat that swarm attack on aircraft. It doesn't even have to have explosives. Aircraft move fast enough that heavy damage is inflicted by what is basically a rock sitting still in the sky. . . .

I don't care how "totally cool" anybody thinks it is to have drones deliver a pizza. It's not worth it. As for Amazon stuff from [Jeff] Bezos? Excuse me?

Books and other hard goods use the existing delivery systems. FedEx, UPS [United Parcel Service] and the USPS [US Postal Service] are very energy efficient per package. Setting up a ridiculously high-energy use way to drop a book on your doorstep is dumb.

Brian Hanley,
"The Problem with Amazon's Drones:
Dangerous and They Disturb the Peace,"
International Policy Digest, July 9, 2014.

ily available though, one Amazon drone-driven death is bound to be viewed as one too many.

3: When it's all said and done, autonomous drones can't do complex jobs, or adapt, as well as people.

Litmus test: Would you ever fly in an airplane that didn't have a pilot on board, but instead was flown wheels-up to wheels-down by a real-live person?

Some people would say "yes," but most people know the value of a real pilot (or pilots) is in being there to solve problems that aren't programmed or put into an algorithm.

Well, surprise! Amazon's airborne ferries are intended to be unmanned and unpiloted.

That might be OK in the controlled setting of, say, the parking lot of Amazon's R&D [research and development] center. It would be a little unnerving, however, to know that unmanned and unpiloted Amazon drones made regular passes over the playground of your kids' school.

There's a reason people still do exceedingly important and potentially dangerous jobs—people remain better at them than computers.

Or, think about it like this.

Delivery drones can't ring a doorbell, retrieve a signature or nestle a package behind a storm door on a rainy day. But Amazon's deliveries are primarily going to be metropolitan areas, mostly to apartment buildings and office buildings? That's even worse. How's the service going to do any better than drop the parcel at the front door of what's apt to be a very big and well-trafficked building?

Bottom Line

Amazon drones face a host of problems in addition to what's been mentioned above. A few other serious considerations include a litany of regulatory hurdles, as well as what happens when people start trying to knock these drones down for their payloads.

Amazon might have gotten some flashy PR [publicity], and probably rankled the likes of FedEx and UPS [United Parcel Service]. But you won't have to start watching the skies for Amazon octocopters anytime soon.

Periodical and Internet Sources Bibliography

The following articles have been selected to supplement the diverse views presented in this chapter.

Evan Ackerman	"When Drone Delivery Makes Sense," *IEEE Spectrum*, September 25, 2014.
Sara Angeles	"8 Reasons to Fear Cloud Computing," Business News Daily, October 1, 2013.
Charles Arthur	"Google Glass: Is It a Threat to Our Privacy?," *Guardian*, March 6, 2013.
Whitney Erin Boesel	"Google Glass Doesn't Have a Problem. You Do," *Time*, May 19, 2014.
Louis Columbus	"Why Cloud Computing Is Slowly Winning the Trust War," *Forbes*, March 12, 2013.
Heather Kelly	"Google Glass Users Fight Privacy Fears," CNN, December 12, 2013.
Gene Marks	"7 Reasons Amazon Drones Are the Dumbest Idea I've Ever Heard," *Philadelphia*, December 3, 2013.
Chris Matyszczyk	"Google Exec: It's 'Irresponsible' of Apple to Make Everything Expensive," CNET, February 26, 2015.
Lucas Mearian	"No, Your Data Isn't Secure in the Cloud," *Computerworld*, August 13, 2013.
Alyssa Newcomb	"From 'Glassholes' to Privacy Issues: The Troubled Run of the First Edition of Google Glass," ABC News, January 16, 2015.
Seth Rosenblatt	"Google, Microsoft Agree: Cloud Is Now Safe Enough to Use," CNET, February 26, 2014.

CHAPTER 3

What Are Some Common Criticisms of Tech Giants?

Chapter Preface

The common criticisms of tech giants extend far beyond the products and services they offer. As large corporate entities, most tech giants also face criticism of their business practices. Many of big tech's detractors argue that companies such as Microsoft, Google, and Amazon sometimes engage in nefarious business practices that stifle competitiveness in their respective marketplaces and are detrimental to the economy and innovation in general. While some of these criticisms involve the entire tech industry and others vary from company to company, they are all indicative of the pitfalls that sometimes come with corporations as big and powerful as today's tech giants.

The business practices for which tech giants are often criticized can come in many forms. One of the most common criticisms of the biggest tech giants is that they have evolved into monopolies. Many critics believe that these tech giants have grown so large and so powerful that they have become all but impossible to compete against and, as a result, are ultimately stifling innovation. Other forms of big tech criticism relate to specific, allegedly dubious, business practices, such as Amazon's effort to provide storefronts for small businesses through Amazon Marketplace. Although this may seem beneficial for small businesses on the surface, critics allege that these businesses are putting themselves at great risk by hitching themselves to Amazon rather than building their own brands.

Another aspect of the modern tech industry that has been the subject of criticism is the practice of "acqui-hiring," in which a tech company acquires talent and ideas by simply buying out a smaller competitor. While some believe that acqui-hires are good for the tech industry, others say the practice is ultimately harmful. Supporters argue that acqui-hiring provides larger companies with a valuable avenue for acquiring the skilled workers they need to ensure continued success. Critics, on the other hand, argue that this approach only serves to reduce competition and stifle innovation, in part because acquiring companies tend to be more interested in the people who work for the companies they acquire than in the products and ideas those companies have developed.

As is the case with other large-scale industries, tech giants' business practices are a critical part of the tech industry to which close attention must be paid. Understanding how tech giants operate provides the ability to ensure that these large corporations continue to do business fairly and ethically so as to maintain a healthy, competitive economic marketplace.

The practice of acqui-hiring is one of the topics discussed in the following chapter, which focuses on the common criticisms of tech giants. Other issues explored include third-party retailers' effect on small business and whether tech giants are monopolistic.

> *"Somebody needs to say it: Google is getting too big. When one organization controls so much of the infrastructure of the digital economy, it's not good for consumers."*

Google Is Monopolistic

Wade Roush

In the following viewpoint, Wade Roush argues that Google is growing so big and powerful that it is quickly becoming a dangerous monopoly. He contends that Google's overly pervasive reach has made the company a detriment to innovation and a threat to our personal freedom. He believes that unchecked ambition has turned Google into an empire that exerts undue control over modern society through its vast array of tech products and services. Roush is a contributing editor with Xconomy and a longtime technology writer whose work has appeared in such publications as Science, MIT Technology Review, *and* IEEE Spectrum.

As you read, consider the following questions:

1. According to Roush, how many acquisitions did Google make between 2010 and early 2014?

2. Why do most big tech companies ultimately end up stifling innovation, according to the viewpoint?

3. According to Roush, why is Google a major target for hackers?

Somebody needs to say it: Google is getting too big. When one organization controls so much of the infrastructure of the digital economy, it's not good for consumers. And when it has such an outsized influence on the resources flowing to inventors, programmers, and entrepreneurs, it's not good for innovation.

Like almost everyone else I know, I'm a heavy user of Google services and technology. Unlike most other people I know, I report on Google as part of my job. So I think about the company a lot. And I worry that the future in store for us—if Google gets a pass from regulators and consumers and continues on its path of insatiable growth—will be a lot more monochromatic than the company's colorful logo.

Google Is Getting Too Big

The news this week [in January 2014] that Google has acquired Nest Labs for north of $3 billion in cash was my personal tipping point. I'm looking at Google and starting to feel that this Silicon Valley success story—and the resulting concentration of wealth, brainpower, and ambition, not to mention data—has gone too far. It's time for consumers, politicians, regulators, journalists like myself, and members of the innovation community to start pushing back on the company.

Google has many vocal critics, and in a way I'm late to the party. For years, I dismissed the concerns of groups like FairSearch, a coalition of Google competitors alleging that Google's behavior in the search marketplace is anticompetitive. Because FairSearch's membership includes companies like Microsoft and Expedia that have their own search businesses, the message always sounded to me like sour grapes.

But now my worries go beyond Google's 67 percent U.S. market share in search (compared to Bing's 18 percent and Yahoo's 11 percent—November 2013 figures). The number that really bothers me is $56.5 billion. That's the amount of cash Google had on hand at the end of the third quarter of 2013. It's the fuel for a series of acquisitions that threaten to undermine market-driven innovation and consolidate a huge chunk of Silicon Valley's engineering talent under a single corporate roof.

Google isn't any more acquisitive now than it always has been—in fact, the pace has slowed a little since the peak year of 2010, when it bought 26 companies. (There were 25 acquisitions in 2011; 11 in 2012; 17 in 2013; and two so far this year [2014] that we know about.) No, the notable change is that Google seems to be thinking more imperially about the sectors it wants to explore.

The Google Empire

When the company was younger, most of its acquisitions related to its core businesses of search, advertising, network infrastructure, and communications. More recently, it's been colonizing areas with a less obvious connection to search—such as travel, social networking, productivity, logistics, energy, and robotics. On top of the M&A [mergers and acquisitions] activity, Google is investing in areas like wearable computing, self-driving cars, and global wireless Internet connectivity via balloons through its Google X skunkworks division, and in longevity-enhancing technologies through its new life sciences subsidiary, Calico.

Think about it. Some morning in the not-too-distant future, you could be awakened by the alarm on your Google-designed phone (Motorola's Moto X) running a Google operating system (Android). You could ride to work in a Google-powered robot car guided by Google-owned GPS [global positioning system] maps (Waze). At your office you'll log onto your Google (Chrome OS) laptop running a Google (Chrome) browser. You'll spend your day analyzing documents and spreadsheets saved on Google's cloud service (Drive) and stay in touch with your coworkers and friends using Google's email system (Gmail) and social network (Google+).

The virtual personal assistant on your phone will stand ready to help you with any question instantaneously (Google Now), and if you miss a call from somebody while it's doing that, they can leave a message on your Google answering service (Voice). At lunch you'll choose a place to eat using Google's restaurant guide (Zagat), make a reservation and get directions by talking to your wearable display (Glass), and pay using your smartphone (Wallet).

When you get home at night, your house's HVAC [heating, ventilation, and air-conditioning] system will adjust itself to your presence using its Google-powered thermostat (Nest) and you'll cook dinner under the watchful eye of your Google-powered smoke alarm (also Nest). You'll eat in front of your Google-powered television (Chromecast) watching shows hosted or licensed by Google (YouTube, Google Play). Before dozing off, you'll pop a Google-funded pill to optimize your metabolism (Calico) and use your tablet (Android) to read a few pages of the latest mystery novel (Google Play again).

And throughout the day, of course, everything you read, watch, search for, and talk about will be tracked by Google's algorithms—the better to show you the targeted ads that generate the high click-through rates that bring in the advertising dollars that subsidize everything else about Google's business.

That's only the beginning. Who knows what master plan for our future is behind Google's recent string of acquisitions in robotics—namely Schaft, Industrial Perception, Redwood Robotics, Meka Robotics, Holomni, Bot & Dolly, Boston Dynamics, and Nest (which is a robotics company at its core, and has a famed academic roboticist, Yoky Matsuoka, as its vice president of technology). John Markoff at the *New York Times* quotes experts who think the big vision behind Google's robotics rollup is about supply-chain automation and robotic delivery men.

To be honest, I don't see any coherent plan. I just see Google waking up to the fact that robots—the hardware that lets software extend its reach in the real world—are the next big technology frontier after the Internet, and deciding to plant its flag.

So, why should it pain me to see so many cool companies, in robotics and other fields, being annexed by Google?

After all, when Google buys a start-up, there's usually a nice financial outcome for the founders and the shareholders. (A *very* nice outcome, in Nest's case; venture backer Kleiner Perkins Caufield & Byers will reportedly see a 20x return on its investment.) Some of that money might eventually get reinvested in new start-ups. And you could argue that joining Google extends an acquired start-up's product-development runway, while freeing its employees from practical business concerns. As long as the AdWords engine keeps pumping out cash—the way a quasar at the center of a distant galaxy spews radio energy—no one else at Google need worry about money. . . .

Giant Companies Are Where Innovation Goes to Die

There's just no way around this truth. For reasons that Clayton Christensen and others have documented, it's extremely difficult for a company that has hatched one world-changing product to keep innovating into its second, third, or fourth decade—Apple being one of the few big counterexamples. After an initial era of exponential innovation and growth (which, for Google, ended about 10 years ago), successful companies get addicted to their cash source, become fearful of internal disruption, and switch to innovation by accretion.

And while Google has a better track record than most companies when it comes to integrating newly acqui-hired employees into its corporate culture, it's not so great at making use of the technologies it buys. Out of the 140-some companies Google has acquired since 2001, only a handful have made notable contributions to the bottom line and the company's overall value. Those include Android (2005), YouTube (2006), DoubleClick (2007), AdMob (2009), and Motorola (2011). And also, perhaps, tiny Upstartle (2006)—this was the company behind Writely, which became Google Docs, which became the core of Google Apps.

As a journalist who loves writing about start-ups and their struggles and triumphs, I'm always a little sad to see the companies I've covered disappear inside Google. I'd point, for example, to Bump Technologies, a Y Combinator company whose mobile app allowed users to exchange business-card data and other files by physically tapping their smartphones together. Bump had some momentum, but it got acquired by Google in September, and a couple of weeks ago the Bump team announced they're shutting down the service in order to focus on "new projects."

Then there's Apture, which helped publishers enhance Web pages (also gone); Wavii, a news aggregator covered by my colleague Ben Romano (gone); and The Fridge, which offered private social networks as an alternative to Facebook (gone).

Once a start-up is absorbed by Google, two crucial things happen. First, the founders and employees cash out their ownership stakes and stock options. They become much wealthier, in theory, but there's no longer much incentive to work start-up hours, take big risks, or pour their lives into their product (assuming it hasn't been discontinued) the way they did when it was just them against the world.

Second, all market pressures are removed. Desktop and mobile search are so enormously profitable for Google that

The Google Monopoly

If "big data" is the oil of the information economy, Google has Standard Oil–like monopoly dominance— and uses that control to maintain its dominant position. Google currently receives 95 percent of all search advertising revenue, the largest component of online advertising, and the marketplace is unlikely to change that absent strong antitrust intervention.

Nathan Newman,
"Taking on Google's Monopoly Means Regulating Its
Control of User Data," Huffington Post, *September 24, 2013.*

there is only a tiny chance that any other product will ever generate a fraction as much revenue. So, again assuming that the start-up's product isn't discontinued, it instantly becomes a hobby rather than a business. That's not a great position to be in, if you really want to innovate and test yourself against the market.

I can't say what will happen to Nest now that it's part of Google. Founder Tony Fadell says the company will retain its brand identity and that, with Google's scale and resources, it will simply be able to get its thermostats and smoke alarms into consumers' hands faster. "Google will help us fully realize our vision of the conscious home," he said in a blog post this week [in January 2014]. "We've had great momentum, but this is a rocket ship."

But frankly, that's what every founder-CEO [chief executive officer] says after they've sold their baby to Google (or any big company). The real questions are 1) whether Nest will feel the pressure to keep innovating that comes from a dwindling bank account—the real fuel for most start-ups' rocket journeys—and 2) whether Nesters will now start thinking more like Googlers.

Nest promised in its original venture pitch deck that "after the thermostat, we're going to reimagine every unloved product in people's lives." But that's not a very Googley sentiment. If anything, it's Appley. I can't help thinking that the Google rewrite of Nest's promise will be something more like: "We're going to make every house into part of a global sensor network, the better to organize the world's information and make it universally accessible and useful." If your future home is conscious, in other words, it will be Google doing the thinking.

We Don't Need a New Ministry of Information

There are obviously some big reasons to appreciate Google: It's full of smart people, and it makes our lives easier and more productive by helping us communicate and find information when we need it. But these services aren't free. We pay in the form of our attention and the data we reveal—through our online and, increasingly, our off-line behavior—about our desires and intentions.

And that brings me to my second big concern about Google's growth. At a time when our privacy is being assaulted from so many directions—by marketers, by hackers and thieves, by our own national security establishment—it feels like a bad idea to allow one company access to so much of this personal information. As Google expands into mobile, entertainment, transportation, robotics, and other markets, it will only want to hoover up more and more of our data, heightening the chances that somebody will want to misuse it.

My worry is that any sufficiently advanced search, communications, and sensing infrastructure is indistinguishable from Big Brother—especially when it's subject to warrantless intrusions by the NSA [National Security Agency]. Granted, Google and its peers have expressed outrage about NSA efforts that allegedly collected millions of emails and other records every day by tapping the fiber-optic cables linking its data centers. And they say they're adding new layers of encryption that may, for now, stymie U.S. and U.K. snooping programs. But simply by centralizing so much data about consumers and businesses, Google will remain an irresistible magnet for hackers, whether they're wearing white hats, black hats, or gray ones.

Google's Moon Shots

From all outward appearances, Google's own intentions are benign. Larry Page, Sergey Brin, and Eric Schmidt seem to me like good guys. But in recent years, Google has developed the somewhat grandiose habit of describing its big investments and R&D initiatives as "moon shots." That's a telling phrase. It connotes not just a willingness to take on hard problems and a tolerance for risk, but a Cold War–era will to dominate—to be the first and the biggest.

If no one but Google has the cash or the courage to pursue big, audacious goals like extending our life spans or photographing every foot of every street on Earth or populating our homes and freeways with robots, then perhaps Google deserves the credit and the eventual spoils. But everyone forgets that the United States' real moon shot—Project Apollo—was so expensive that the last three missions had to be canceled. (As a first step into the solar system, Apollo was awkward and abortive. Who's on the moon today? A Chinese rover.)

Moon shots staged by superpowers who've drafted every available brain aren't the right way to organize sustainable innovation and economic growth. That takes a balance of collaboration and competition, free market enterprise and regulation, ambition and humility. It's time for Google to come back down to Earth.

> "*The world's top search firm may be many things—some of which aren't pretty—but an illegal monopoly, it is not.*"

Google Is Not Monopolistic

Ryan Radia

In the following viewpoint, Ryan Radia argues that Google is not, in fact, a monopoly as many of its critics claim. Radia instead contends that many of the things that people cite when alleging that Google is a monopoly, such as having a so-called "search bias," is just the nature of how a business like Google works and is not indicative of any monopolistic tendencies. Further, he says that Google really is not any different than any other tech company of its kind. Radia is an associate director of technology studies at the Competitive Enterprise Institute in Washington, DC.

As you read, consider the following questions:

1. According to Radia, why are claims that Google is guilty of "search bias" inaccurate?

2. Why is there no chance of a serious antitrust case against Google, according to the viewpoint?

3. According to Radia, what are American antitrust laws designed to do, and how does this inherently preclude Google from being considered a monopoly?

The Internet market is notoriously dynamic. Its giants rise and fall far faster than their brick-and-mortar counterparts. This dynamism perplexes and worries many—especially regulators in Washington, D.C.

Perhaps no Internet leader faces as much scrutiny from government as Google, which has been the subject of a Federal Trade Commission [FTC] antitrust probe for over a year. As this investigation comes to a close, the government is reportedly leaning toward suing Google before year's end. Naturally, its rivals are lobbying the feds to come down hard on the search giant.

Yet Google's critics haven't put forward a serious legal case against the company. The world's top search firm may be many things—some of which aren't pretty—but an illegal monopoly, it is not. If the feds haul Google to court, they'll send Silicon Valley a powerful message: Washington is open for business and happy to meddle with the Internet economy.

The Search Bias Fallacy

Perhaps the most commonly recited complaint against Google is that its search results are biased toward the company's own offerings—such as its product search and maps—to the detriment of its competitors. Some specialized search engines, such as Foundem (a price comparison service) complain they're inexplicably ranked poorly by Google search, even as Google's own specialized search engine appears prominently in the results.

Before unpacking this argument, it's worth noting every attempt to show Google suffers from rampant "search bias" has fallen flat.

A 2011 study by Harvard professor Ben Edelman—perhaps the most prominent analysis of search bias to date—

purported to find that Google linked to its own properties in its search results more than three times as often as do other search engines. But more recently, a vastly more extensive study by George Mason University's Joshua Wright found Edelman's methodology to be "designed to maximize the incidence of search bias." So Wright analyzed a bigger data set and found Google rarely ranks its own content higher than rival search engines do. It turns out that Bing, Google's chief rival, actually displays alleged search bias nearly twice as often as Google.

Admittedly, measuring bias in search is tricky, as Google founders Larry Page and Sergey Brin explained in a 1998 Stanford [University] working paper. If a search engine is covertly preferring its top advertisers in the "organic" rankings, users may never find out.

But nobody is accusing Google of selling search priority to the highest bidders. Rather, critics like Edelman merely claim Google's search engine treats the company's products somewhat more favorably than rival search engines do.

Does this mean Google is biased? Not really—at least, no more so than its competitors. There is, after all, no "unbiased" baseline against which to compare every search engine. If anything, search is all about competing biases. Search engines compete by striving to give users better results than they can get from rivals.

A search engine's job is to answer each query by generating links that best match the user's search term. This task is enormously challenging; deciding which website best "answers" a particular search query is as subjective a question as they come.

How do search engines decide which results to generate for each query and how to order them? For one thing, they may measure each site's popularity. If most users who search for "email" go on to Yahoo Mail, for instance, it could mean Yahoo Mail is the best result.

But if searching the web were simply a popularity contest, all search engines would return nearly identical results. They certainly wouldn't employ teams of computer scientists to constantly tweak their search algorithms.

In reality, however, a website's popularity is only one of hundreds of signals that search engines use to generate results. An awesome new gaming website that few users have yet discovered may merit a higher search ranking than older—but more widely trafficked—gaming sites. A search engine's challenge is to sort through the trillion websites out there and decide how best to weigh the many factors behind each site's ranking.

Back to search bias: Why, in 2011, did a Google search for "email" return Gmail first—and Yahoo Mail second—even though far more users actually selected the latter option?

Maybe Google was out to cripple Yahoo by forcing its own inferior products on users. More likely, however, Google simply thought Gmail was a better answer than Yahoo Mail. After all, Google spent years building a product it hoped would revolutionize email by offering unique features (such as gigabytes of free storage.)

Google's critics obsess over the inner workings of the company's search algorithm, known as Google's "secret sauce." Conspiracy theories abound regarding Google's alleged manipulation of search results. Why would Google demote my website, the argument usually goes, unless it's out to get me?

But what really matters is whether Google's algorithm is doing its job: generating results that users believe best answer their searches. This effort entails frequent tweaks, and occasionally causes some websites' rankings to drop dramatically. For instance, in April 2012, Google unveiled the "Penguin" update to punish low-quality websites. And in September, Google began demoting websites that frequently generate copyright complaints.

Google Is Not a Monopoly

Google dominates the search market. Not only do 60+ percent of web searches happen on Google, but it's so dominant in people's minds that "to google" has entered the lexicon as shorthand for "search the Internet." . . . For a large number of people, Google *is* the Internet; it's where you go to see the websites. I think I can safely say that more than a few people literally think that the Internet is stored inside Google somewhere. But it's not. It's that kind of thinking that makes people think that Google has a monopoly. . . .

No matter how much better Google's search is, or how much more popular it is, those facts alone will never make it a monopoly. If I were to invent a new flavor of ice cream that was so good . . . and people stopped buying all the other kinds of ice cream, I still wouldn't have a monopoly on ice cream. I would just be a very rich guy with an awesome secret ice cream recipe. I would only have a monopoly on ice cream if I abused my market position to artificially make other kinds of ice cream unavailable.

David Adams,
"Google Does Not Have a Monopoly on Search,"
OSNews, February 25, 2010.

Even Google's own properties aren't immune from these demotions; in early 2012, when Chrome violated Google's paid links policy, its search ranking plummeted.

Google undoubtedly makes the wrong call sometimes, to be sure; not every tweak works out for the better. But these mistakes are inevitable when search engines are coded by human beings.

Where's the Harm?

The secrecy surrounding Google's search algorithm makes it impossible to know just how it decides to rank each website. (It also makes it tough for spammers to game Google's system, though not for lack of trying.)

Google's critics say it can't be trusted to overcome the irresistible temptation to "abuse" its search dominance. They point to Page and Brin's 1998 academic paper, in which they admit "search engine bias is particularly insidious" and tough to detect. Thus, critics argue, the only way to ensure Google acts in users' interests is by government bureaucrats peering over its shoulder—and examining the recipe for its secret sauce.

For all we know, Google may well routinely manipulate search results in a self-serving manner. If it does, would users notice the degraded results? Would they flee to other search engines such as Bing and AOL, or specialized search sites such as Amazon or Twitter?

Absolutely, Google argues. "Competition," it often says, "is one click away."

Bolstering this argument is Microsoft's recent blind search engine "taste test," in which 5 million visitors preferred Bing to Google by a two-to-one margin.

But even if Google critics are right, and the company could abuse its dominance, where is the evidence that it has? Where is the evidence that Google's efforts to improve search quality have harmed consumers?

Without such evidence, there is no serious antitrust case against Google. It's perfectly legal for a company to compete by serving its users, no matter how high its market share or how much its rivals suffer as a result. As the Supreme Court has explained, a company with monopoly power is generally free to compete however it wishes, so long as it has "legitimate competitive reasons" for its actions. What could be more legitimate than trying to deliver better search results?

There's also no evidence that Google's conduct has choked off rivals. In fact, as the *Daily Caller* reported in September 2012, many of Google's "victims" appear to be thriving.

Yelp's CEO reported massive growth in use of its mobile app during an August earnings call. And in July, TripAdvisor's CEO told investors not to worry about Google because his company was "entrenched in the fabric of travel planning."

So much for Google "tend[ing] to destroy competition itself," to borrow a phrase from a Supreme Court opinion explaining the purpose of antitrust laws.

To Google's critics, however, any evidence of preferential treatment proves Google's guilt. Their argument boils down to the audacious claim that it's illegal for Google's search engine to show preferential treatment to Google products. As punishment, they want the government to forbid Google from deciding that consumers actually might prefer its products and thus rank them prominently in Google search.

But if Google is so powerful that it can trounce rivals and spread its dominance throughout the web virtually unchallenged, why did its much-hyped Wave and Buzz products fall flat? Why does Google+ have a mere 100 million active users versus Facebook's staggering 1 billion users? And why are venture capitalists investing in start-ups more than they ever have since the dot-com bubble's peak in spring 2001?

If Google Is Evil, So Is Everybody Else

In fairness to Google's critics, they are right about one thing: Google is no saint. In fact, it's committed some major screwups over the years. For instance, the company's Street View cars collected wireless "payload data" from some unsecured networks, landing Google in hot water with governments around the world. In early 2010, when Google launched Buzz (the predecessor to Google+) some users' private contacts became publicly visible. Within days, Google apologized for the mistake and fixed it—but still ended up paying $8.5

million in a class-action settlement. And last August, Google paid an unprecedented $500 million fine to settle claims its employees had helped Canadian pharmacies illegally peddle medicine to U.S. consumers.

Yet, troubling as these actions may be, they do not make Google an illegal monopoly. If they did, Google's rivals would be in hot water, too. Nearly every major multinational corporation has run afoul of at least one law or regulation—often several times. Just as Google is subject to a 20-year consent decree with the FTC over alleged privacy violations, so are Facebook, Twitter, Microsoft, and Myspace (to name just a few examples).

As much as Google is disliked in some circles, America's antitrust laws are designed not to punish companies for growing too big or too unpopular, but to ensure no company stifles competition itself. The thriving Internet sector—a bright spot in America's otherwise lackluster economy—shows no signs of suffering from too little competition. While all markets are decidedly imperfect, antitrust litigation is ill-equipped to distinguish beneficial innovation from the harmful kind, as scholars Geoffrey Manne and Joshua Wright explained in a 2011 *Harvard Journal of Law and Public Policy* article.

Nobel Prize–winning economist Ronald Coase once quipped that when "an economist finds . . . a business practice . . . he does not understand, he looks for a monopoly explanation." This sums up the fallacy underlying the case against Google. Its behavior may be frustrating, its employees fallible, and its products inconsistent—but it's also an American success story that has changed the world for the better, following in the footsteps of Ford, Sears, General Electric, Apple, Amazon, and even Microsoft.

In Silicon Valley, brilliant ideas breed success, and entrepreneurs expand our economic pie by creating wealth. Washington, by contrast, revolves around influence peddling, special interest lobbying, and zero-sum rent-seeking games. If we want the Internet to remain dynamic, vibrant, and unpredictable, the government needs to leave it alone.

> *"The acqui-hire and overall [merger and acquisition] trend is the reason behind my conviction that the next big company will be founded by someone who is currently working at one of Silicon Valley's top tech companies."*

Today's Acqui-Hires Will Become Tomorrow's Innovators

Peter Relan

In the following viewpoint, Peter Relan argues that acqui-hiring is a beneficial practice in the tech industry that will only help to encourage further innovation. He explains what acqui-hiring is and asserts that this practice offers bright young tech employees the opportunity to be the next big success story in the constantly evolving tech field. He contends that acqui-hires are good for both tech workers and the tech industry as a whole. Relan is a successful Silicon Valley entrepreneur and the founder of YouWeb Incubator.

As you read, consider the following questions:

1. According to the viewpoint, what are acqui-hires?

2. Why do tech companies engage in acqui-hiring, according to Relan?

3. According to Relan, how do acqui-hired individuals benefit from working for larger tech companies?

There is no doubt about the unprecedented wealth of talent in Silicon Valley, both technical and entrepreneurial. The area has become known as a mecca, and for some the Wild West, of digital innovation. So many entrepreneurs migrate to the valley in hopes of building the next Facebook or Twitter, and technical talent and engineers are the bread and butter making this possible.

Most of the engineers that come out here after finishing school or graduating from local universities like Stanford [University] or [the University of California,] Berkeley have the desire, at some point, to start their own companies. Most of these engineers, however, will find this a daunting task better left for a few years down the road and seek to find their bearings by joining a small but promising start-up.

This wealth of talent has led to an idea that you've certainly heard a lot about by now: the acqui-hire, the acquisition of a company purely for its talent. Yahoo, Google, Twitter and Facebook are the main companies behind acqui-hires and overall acquisitions over the last couple of years, which has led to many young start-ups, alongside their handful of rock star engineers, being gobbled up into a new organizational structure.

Make no mistake—even successful M&A [merger and acquisition] deals often leave VCs [venture capitalists] and founders well compensated. But other senior and mid-level team members are often hungry for more, having tasted some success but are nowhere near ready to retire. Thus, the next Jack Dorsey is probably already in Silicon Valley but is not currently an entrepreneur. Rather, they are biding their time working within a bigger tech titan, dreaming about something bigger.

It seems an innocuous enough practice, but the acqui-hire and overall M&A trend is the reason behind my conviction that the next big company will be founded by someone who is currently working at one of Silicon Valley's top tech companies, but who may never have been a founder themselves.

Here's Why

What's unique about this moment in Silicon Valley history is the sheer number of engineers in companies like these that have been brought in through acquisitions, or the increasingly popular acqui-hire. Big companies will acquire smaller, hungrier start-ups that have great teams with great talent and put these minds to work on existing initiatives. Tim Cook has even publicly stated that this has been Apple's strategy—to bring in companies that not only contribute a product but a superior team to add value—and it has averaged an acquisition almost every other month for three years.

I've been running an incubator for six years, and I've observed something interesting. While Peter Thiel's 20 under 20 program is fascinating and holds promise, and Y Combinator has a great track record for bringing young entrepreneurs to Silicon Valley, there is an untapped group of potential founders who are milling about right under our noses. These individuals, likely engineers and product managers in their late 20s or early 30s, have hard skills working at a start-up, an understanding of the market, and are drawn to entrepreneurship but are slightly more risk averse.

These future founders may not have track records as the founders or CEOs [chief executive officers] of companies with exits, but they have worked for a start-up *and* now a large company. They understand what it means to build a product, and they also understand what scale looks and feels like now

Acquirer	Select Recent Acquihires	
Facebook	Storylane	Long-form Blogging Platform
	Threadsy	Integrated Social Platform
	Lightbox	Social Photo - Android
	Hotspots.io	Social Analytics
Twitter	RestEngine	Email Marketing
	Cabana	Visual App Design
	MileWise	Consumer Frequent Flyer Miles
Yahoo	Loki Studios	Mobile Gaming
	Ptch	Social Discovery Platform

TAKEN FROM: CB Insights, "The Rise of the Acqui-hire: Breaking Down Talent Acquisitions," January 9, 2014.

that they have worked at Facebook, Yahoo, Twitter or Google. You need both for the maximum probability of success in building The Next Big Thing.

Many entrepreneurs have seen the former—it's the easier part—and it's why Y Combinator is able to pull 50+ companies a class with the seeds of a product already built. Where many entrepreneurs fail, however, is during the scaling stage, as it's very difficult to get it right if you haven't seen it done before. Of course, other types of founders can succeed, too, but the maximum probability of success is in this type of founder.

The Company Matters

When I say, "working for a company that is highly innovative," I mean companies like Google, Twitter and Facebook. Google because it has an agenda, which, as Larry Page put it, is "to build great things that don't exist"; Facebook because it has the highly iterative hack-and-break things mentality; and Twitter because it's had to innovate a lot to figure out its monetization models.

Google and Facebook are examples of companies that truly stand apart from the rest and empower their employees, but in slightly different ways—one being a corporate goliath with high ideals to change the world, and the other a big start-up that is constantly thinking of better ways to optimize and re-engineer an idea. Yahoo is getting there, as well, under Marissa Mayer. It's why many founders have come from these companies, including Pinterest founder Ben Silbermann who worked in customer support and sales for Google, when he decided to leave to start his own venture. It's not that Ben did not like Google, but just as most entrepreneurs, he wanted more.

Another example of a team being acquired, working for their acquirer, and then breaking out to develop their own companies are members from the former AdMob team, which was acquired by Google in 2009. Two members of this team who went on to found companies of their own were Kamakshi Sivaramakrishnan, who founded self-learning, cross-device ad company Drawbridge, and Mike Mettler, founder of Card.io, which was acquired last year by PayPal. This is a great example of two entrepreneurs working from the ground up, seeing and feeling what scale truly feels like, who went into bigger companies and decided that they had what it took to build their own companies. And it worked.

What's unique about both Facebook and Google is the fact that both have a bottom-up, technically driven culture where they designate a specific amount of time for employees to work on projects they like, encouraging the engineers to take time to work creatively on new, non-initiative products that can spur creativity and new ideas or approaches that might not have otherwise been pursued.

I had lunch with a founder that came out of my incubator that was recently acquired by Facebook, and he had nothing but the highest praise for the hacker way of the entire company and how it works there. In his essay "The Hacker Way,"

Mark Zuckerberg defines a hacker as a person who is never finished with their work, believing that there is always room for improvement no matter what the product. This is the vision of the CEO. This is how the company is run, and, for the most part, this is how the majority of the engineers at Facebook feel and operate.

Imagine this situation: You worked for a start-up for a year or two, you've gone through an acquisition (or acqui-hire) and you now are settled (more than you probably would like to be) in this big company. You've been there a year or two and you were then asked to come up with an "intrapreneur" project that you want to drive to scale. What if, as an engineer at Google, you use your weekly 20 percent time to develop and create an idea or product that you're incredibly passionate about. What better training can you possibly get to be a future founder?

Now add the second ingredient: accelerators popping up everywhere. Despite my prediction that most will fail to do well for their investors, I add that they are great for the U.S. and the world. Well-trained future founders with access to seed capital and mentorship equals a great recipe for creating start-ups.

While Google, Facebook and Twitter do a fantastic job of acquiring and then retaining rock star engineers at their bottom-up, technically driven companies, I predict it will be these specific folks who will drive the next evolution of Silicon Valley. Their experience within an innovative big company, coupled with their amazing network and time to think about a problem/solution while being paid a nice salary, makes for the best recipe to build something that succeeds. It is on the heels of this trend that the next Jack Dorsey, Elon Musk or Steve Jobs will appear.

> "The ideas—not just the people—are getting acquired. . . . Instead of 'acqui-hires,' they're really 'innovation-quisitions.'"

Tech Giants Stifle Innovation with Acqui-Hires

Robert Hatta

In the following viewpoint, Robert Hatta argues that acqui-hires are detrimental to the tech industry and innovation within that industry. He contends that acqui-hires, because of their effect on many of the tech industry's most promising talent, stifle creativity and innovation far more than they help to cultivate it. Further, he worries that if this trend continues, the tech industry will ultimately suffer. Hatta is a talent partner at Drive Capital and an expert in technology and entrepreneurialism.

As you read, consider the following questions:

1. According to Hatta, what happens to the products and founders of the companies bought out by tech giants through acqui-hires?

2. According to the viewpoint, why are acqui-hires really "innovation-quisitions"?

3. What happens when tech giants acquire outside talent but fail to promote creativity and innovation, according to Hatta?

It's hard to talk about a tech bubble these days (and it's hard *not* to talk about a tech bubble these days) without spending some time ranting or raving about the latest trend in talent acquisition: the so-called "acqui-hire," which occurs when a tech company is perceived to be buying a young business not for its products or its customers, but for its talent. The products, if there are any, are often scrapped just as the golden handcuffs are slapped on the start-up's founders and key personnel.

Google, Zynga and Facebook have made headlines for their recent "acqui-hires," sucking up engineering talent like Mega Maid in *Spaceballs*. When six-figure salaries straight out of undergrad, state-of-the-art equipment and free haircuts aren't enough to attract top talent, just go buy a company with some smart people and add them to your payroll, the thinking goes.

But when you break it down, the per-head cost of these types of acquisitions is typically $1 million or more. And that doesn't take into account the many hours of market analysis and due diligence performed by the acquiring company's corporate development team, along with the commensurate legal and transactional costs that go into even a small deal.

Acquiring Businesses for Profit, Not Talent

Established companies acquire other businesses to grow their revenue, lower costs, enter new markets, or add on strategically important features, products or services. Growth companies are no different. Rarely, if ever, does a company set out to purchase another just to acquire a person or a group of people, like a headhunter or a recruiter would do.

I spoke to a friend who works in corporate development for one of the most acquisitive companies in Silicon Valley. He

Acquiring Talent

Many large technology companies have turned to a drastic—but increasingly common—method of recruiting engineering talent: buying start-up companies. . . . In many cases, the buyer has little or no interest in acquiring the company's products, customer relationships or intellectual property. Rather, the prized asset changing hands in the acquisition is people: namely, the start-up's engineering team. In fact, often in these transactions—popularly referred to as "acqui-hires"—the start-up is shut down shortly after the closing of the acquisition, resulting in discontinued products and services and pink slips for non-engineer employees. For faltering start-ups on the road to nowhere, the acqui-hire exit may simply be viewed as a hastening of the inevitable. Still, for other more promising business ventures, these transactions arguably stifle innovation, resulting in the premature abandonment of promising ideas and the undeserved loss of investor capital.

Scott R. Bleier, "The 'Acqui-Hire' Trend:
Issues for Founders and Investors and Drafting Options,"
Morse, Barnes-Brown & Pendleton, October 2012.

said that his employer does not set out to acquire specific people. Rather, they work with their own product teams to identify strategic market or technology areas of interest or of importance. They then look to see what companies are innovating on the cutting edge of those spaces. Sometimes the target companies are so young that they don't even have a commercial product yet, but they are making a name for themselves at trade events and on the fund-raising circuit. If they do have a product in the market, it's rare that the acquirer can integrate it with its platform in a cost-effective way or at the scale required by the acquiring company. So it gets chucked. But the ideas that drove the product remain.

The ideas—not just the people—are getting acquired. While ideas are hard to separate from the people who create them, it's easier to reconcile the aforementioned math when you're talking about the value of ideas. Instead of "acqui-hires," they're really "innovation-quisitions."

And despite being a recently coined term, this is not a new trend or a sign that the tech apocalypse is upon us. For decades, businesses have bought up teams as a way to add capabilities and accelerate entry into strategic and growing markets, according to Brad Wertz, president of interactive agency Rosetta. He should know. Mr. Wertz has been acquired not once, not twice, but four times in the last five years. He ran Xteric Technology Group, a Cleveland-based IT [information technology] services company that was acquired by interactive agency Brulant in 2006. Brulant was purchased by Rosetta two years later. And Rosetta was purchased just last month [in May 2011] by global creative powerhouse Publicis Groupe. According to Mr. Wertz, acquisitions of teams are typical to accelerate entry into new markets where the target company contains people with talent and experience in the desired sector.

Motivating Innovation

Young tech companies are a growth engine of our economy. Groupon alone is hiring 125–150 people a month in only its third year in existence. Can it be good for our country's innovation when these young companies are swallowed by bigger, more established market leaders before they can even launch their new technologies? Are today's innovators selling out too quickly to their deep-pocketed tech overlords who can't seem to hire (or retain) people the old-fashioned way? I don't think so. And neither does Mr. Wertz. "If anything," he says, "it spawns more innovation by motivating people to create new ideas with the promise of a nice payday."

In the larger, but still nimble environment of an acquiring company, newly acquired innovators can have access to far greater resources and a larger customer base through which to accelerate their innovations. However, if the environment at an acquiring company doesn't encourage innovative thinking and entrepreneurial action, the acquired talent is sure to chafe and quickly churn out.

> "*I see both Amazon and eBay as detrimental to any business interested in building its own brand.... They have no interest in helping you build your business (no matter what they say).*"

Third-Party Online Retailers Are Detrimental to Small Business

Jamie Salvatori

In the following viewpoint, Jamie Salvatori argues that third-party online retailers such as Amazon and eBay are more harmful to small businesses than helpful. He contends that Amazon and eBay are ultimately concerned only with their own business and, even though they provide a convenient platform for small businesses to connect with consumers, will always put their own interests first. Further, he suggests that focusing on building a brand is far more effective and reliable than simply depending on making sales through third-party retailers. Salvatori is a small business owner and a computer science expert.

As you read, consider the following questions:

1. According to Salvatori, why is depending on a third-party retailer a recipe for disaster?

2. Why is it difficult for small businesses to get repeat business through third-party retailers, according to the viewpoint?

3. According to Salvatori, why can't small businesses survive only by competing on price?

In business, you must always be on the lookout for so-called black swan events [rare or surprising events that have major effects]. This may seem a bit illogical, but the point is that everything you rely upon in business has the potential to completely upend or destroy your business.

Many years ago, my business sold a driver's educational DVD that we had produced ourselves. We had first released it in the year 2000. It sold very well due to a single high-volume affiliate.

We had a great relationship with one affiliate. He earned a great commission, we sold a lot of DVDs, and everyone was happy. So, in 2006, we set out to update our production. By early 2008, it was ready to be released. We were both looking forward to higher conversion rates and greater profits.

And then all hell broke loose. His business was sued by a state government and he was forced to change his website substantially, causing sales of the DVD to plummet.

The moral of the story is obvious. Don't rely on a single sales channel. This maxim can apply to most areas of your e-commerce business. Don't rely on a single source of traffic. Don't rely on a single supplier of mission critical items. And don't rely on a single employee for any mission critical process (aka know how to do everything yourself in case they disappear one day unexpectedly).

This is precisely why we decided to stop selling on Amazon and eBay. I don't think that Amazon or eBay will cease to exist, but it is inarguable that they exist solely for their own benefit. They do not exist for my benefit.

Third-Party Retailers and Small Businesses

I see both Amazon and eBay as detrimental to any business interested in building its own brand. Amazon and eBay are interested in building Amazon and eBay. They have no interest in helping you build your business (no matter what they say).

At a moment's notice, Amazon could make an operational change that would render your business completely obsolete. You could be selling soap and they could decide to purchase a soap retailer and eliminate all third-party soap listings. It's not that far-fetched.

And what would happen to you if eBay decided to ban the sale of whatever you're pushing? You'd be out of business the next day. So, why would you bother investing in and building a business based upon the whims of another entity that, frankly, has zero vested interest in your specific success? If you disappear, they probably wouldn't notice. But if they disappear, you're screwed. That's not a partnership. That's a recipe for disaster.

You may scoff at my fears (and most people did at the thought of a black swan), so here's another reason to completely abandon all third-party sales channels: repeat business.

The bottom line is that businesses can only exist upon repeat business. You cannot create repeat business on Amazon and eBay because all of the branding is designed to reinforce their sales channel and not your store. Sure, you can *try* gimmicks on eBay like handwritten notes stuffed inside the box, but that's not going to scale beyond a few dozen orders a day. It also can't compete against the fact that the customer remembers making their purchase on eBay and not your seller store.

Therefore, you are reduced to always having to compete on price (which is what the owner of the sales channel wants!). You cannot survive competing solely on price because it doesn't give you a chance to utilize any of your strengths in marketing, merchandising, or customer service. So, don't bother with it! It isn't worth it in the long run.

The Importance of Branding

Nearly all of my posts preach building your own brand. I realize I must sound like a broken record, but any good idea is worth repeating. You cannot build your brand if you're piggybacking on Amazon or eBay. They are a crutch and should be avoided.

Obviously, Amazon and eBay "solve" your biggest problem: traffic. But they also prevent you from building your most important asset: traffic.

If you're serious about building your brand, you must leave eBay and Amazon behind. You'll be far happier once you do. When you first start, your direct traffic will be a small percentage of overall traffic and it will be depressing. So, you'll have to pay for most of your traffic, but eventually, you'll start to earn a following. This is invigorating. They actually remembered my website name!

Plus, direct traffic is a million times better than "free" traffic from SEO [search engine optimization] because it can't disappear due to an algorithm change.

Even if you have a "side" Amazon or eBay store, I recommend shutting them down for a laser-like focus on your domain. The time and effort spent operating these third-party stores is a huge opportunity cost. You'd be far better served funneling that time toward building your own brand.

Investing in your brand is effectively investing in yourself. I'd rather invest in myself than an Amazon, eBay, Facebook, Etsy, Pinterest, or the latest trend in third-party stores.

Periodical and Internet Sources Bibliography

The following articles have been selected to supplement the diverse views presented in this chapter.

Rakesh Agrawal	"How Amazon Can Be a Friend to Small Businesses," VentureBeat, March 19, 2012.
Mark Ames	"Google Wants Us to Forget About Its Near-Total Monopoly over What We Know," *Pando-Daily*, July 3, 2014.
Drake Baer	"Peter Thiel: Google Has Insane Perks Because It's a Monopoly," Business Insider, September 16, 2014.
Jackson Burke	"Have Job, Will Buy Your Firm: Tech's 'Acqui-hire' Trend," CNBC, November 9, 2014.
Frédéric Filloux	"Google Might Not Be a Monopoly, After All," *Monday Note*, June 30, 2014.
Sarah Lacy	"The Acqui-Hire Scourge: Whatever Happened to Failure in Silicon Valley?," *PandoDaily*, August 25, 2012.
Ben Narasin	"The End of the Acqui-Hire?," TechCrunch, May 17, 2014.
Lauren Rae Orsini	"How Amazon Exploits Small Online Retailers," *Daily Dot*, November 1, 2012.
Steven Power	"Why Amazon Is Bad for (Small) Business," *Huffington Post*, June 12, 2013.
Marcus Wohlsen	"Thanks to Amazon, Tiny Sellers Can Now Reach Across the Globe," CNN, September 3, 2014.
Jay Yarow	"Why So Many Startups Are Being Acqui-Hired," Business Insider, August 10, 2012.

OPPOSING
VIEWPOINTS®
SERIES

CHAPTER 4

What Does the Future Hold for Tech Giants?

Chapter Preface

It goes without saying that technology companies are always looking toward the future. Success in the tech industry is often dependent on a company's ability to pioneer new ideas and introduce new technological solutions. Consequently, these companies invest much time and money in researching and developing the latest cutting-edge innovations in hopes of staying one step ahead of their competitors and maintaining their place in the ever changing tech marketplace. Today, big tech is moving at a lightning-fast pace into new endeavors that could have a significant impact on the way people will live, work, and do business in the years to come.

So, what exactly might change if the tech giants are successful in some of their most forward-thinking projects? In some cases, big tech is looking to make the world even more virtually connected than it already is. With its Project Loon venture, Google is planning to bring Internet access to some of the world's most remote regions with the aid of balloons designed to float through the stratosphere and deliver Wi-Fi to the communities below.

Back on the ground, Facebook and other tech companies are weighing the potential benefits of entering the banking industry and offering financial services to rival those currently offered by traditional banks. Facebook recently applied for an e-money license from Ireland's central bank that, if approved, will allow the company to electronically send money throughout Europe. Further, *American Banker* magazine reports that the company has obtained money services business licenses in forty-eight US states. Facebook also began allowing its users to send money to one another free of charge via the site's Messenger app in March 2015.

Banking is not the only outside industry the tech giants are planning to enter, however. One of the most ambitious and interesting ideas some tech companies are currently exploring is entering the automotive industry. A number of tech giants are now in the relatively early stages of developing their own branded vehicles, which they plan to manufacture and sell to the public. Several tech companies, such as Tesla Motors, Google, and NVIDIA Corporation, are working to develop self-driving cars; others, such as Apple, are focusing on perhaps the more realistic prospect of creating and marketing their own electric cars. Fans and critics alike are somewhat divided on whether they think tech companies will ultimately be successful in these endeavors. With respect to self-driving cars, critics often are split on questions such as whether a car that drives itself can ever truly be safe or whether tech companies can overcome the many legal hurdles involved in putting self-driving cars on the road. Further, where simpler branded electric cars are concerned, many critics doubt whether tech companies are really equipped to handle all the realities of manufacturing and selling vehicles—an industry that is quite different from any with which most tech companies are currently familiar.

Regardless of whether any of these projects ever fully come to fruition, it is clear that tech giants will remain on the leading edge of technological innovation. The following chapter discusses future endeavors of the largest technology companies.

"Banks must develop a new knowledge-based business model for the digital world."

Big Tech Poses a Challenge to Traditional Banks

Francisco González

In the following viewpoint, Francisco González argues that tech giants such as Google are poised to take over the banking industry in the years to come. He contends that consumer demand and tech companies' interest in pursuing new business opportunities will lead to a dramatic shift in the banking industry to which traditional banks must begin to adapt. Further, he says that banks that fail to adapt are almost certainly doomed to fail. González is the executive chairman and chief executive officer of Banco Bilbao Vizcaya Argentaria (BBVA) and a banking industry expert.

As you read, consider the following questions:

1. According to González, what percentage of millennials deal with their banks exclusively online?

2. What is a key competitive advantage that traditional banks enjoy, according to the viewpoint?

3. What are the reasons González gives explaining why Google, Facebook, Amazon, and Apple are taking an interest in offering financial services?

In the past few years we have witnessed the far-reaching effects of the ongoing technological revolution on the ways we do business. Individual industries and whole sectors have been transformed; companies seemingly conjured from thin air swiftly rise to the top of their fields, joining the ranks of the world's most valuable businesses. Conversely, long-established industry names fall into decay or disappear altogether. . . .

Technology has changed, shifting the boundaries of production and distribution possibilities. Customers have changed, as have their requirements and the ways in which we reach them. Employees have changed, and their skills and motivation are now different. Change also takes place in organizational structures, decision-making models and forms of leadership, to meet the challenges of today and face those of tomorrow: Technological progress and social development never stop, creating new uncertainties on the horizon of the business world.

These processes of transformation are all the more far-reaching, swift and radical in information-rich domains, such as the media, culture, and entertainment. Banking has changed, too. But despite being an information-rich activity—the "raw materials" of financial services are money and information—banking has changed a lot less than other industries. Money is readily digitized: When it takes the form of electronic book entries, it becomes information that can be processed and transferred in an instant.

Various reasons have been suggested to explain why banking has changed relatively little. First, the industry is subject to heavy regulation and government intervention. This discourages potential new entrants, so incumbent banks feel less pressure to change. Another factor often pointed to is average user age, which is higher than that seen in other industries, such as music. What's more, most people take a conservative approach to their finances. And it may well be that the rapid growth and high earnings of the financial services industry in the years leading up to the downturn nurtured complacency and inefficiencies which in other sectors would have proved fatal.

But all this is changing. In fact, it already has changed. After the downturn, the financial services industry finds itself in an entirely new landscape. Laws and regulations are a lot tougher in the fields of consumer protection, good practice requirements, control, and capital ratios. This means thinner margins, higher costs, and lower earnings. In addition, users are now more demanding—they want improved transparency, cheaper prices and higher service quality.

Only a major effort of transformation will enable banks to return to profit figures capable of assuring medium- and long-term survival, and, by offering a wider, improved range of services at competitive prices, to restore their tarnished reputations in the eyes of customers and society at large.

This transformation is increasingly urgent for two powerful reasons. First, customers are changing swiftly; secondly, new competitors are stepping onto the stage.

A whole generation of customers have grown up with the Internet—they make intensive use of social media and live in a "digital mode." The "millennial" generation . . . are now aged 25 to 40. They are approaching the peak of their professional development and making major financial decisions. By 2020, "millennials" will account for a third of the population of the United States and 75% of the workforce. 90% of them deal with their banks exclusively online, and half of them do so using their smartphones.

Over 70% of millennials say they would be happy to pay for banking products and services provided by non-banking companies—for example, telecommunications operators, technology and Internet providers, online retailers. These percentages exceed 50% even among earlier generations—aged up to 55 years.

What this means is that banks are losing their monopoly over people's financial trust. And later generations—like "Generation Z," born in or after the 1990s—will no doubt bring still greater developments which are yet to be discovered.

The United States is in most respects at the forefront of these changes, but the trend is global. It is not only in developed countries where we can see this shift. In developing countries, too, the more affluent customers are following the same pattern. What's more, technology is making it possible to offer financial products and services to a poorer, more scattered population which conventional banks are unable to cater for at affordable prices. This potential market encompasses up to two billion new customers.

Change is opening up opportunities that foster the rise of a new league of competitors—mostly but not exclusively spilling over from the digital world. These new entrants can be far more efficient and agile than banks, because they are not burdened with inefficient, rigid and largely obsolete technologies or expensive brick-and-mortar distribution networks.

From Analog to Digital: Toward Knowledge-Driven Banking

Today banks must face a tough climate: tighter margins; overcapacity; tarnished reputations; and the pressure of new high-tech competitors who can move flexibly, unburdened by cost legacies.

But banks do enjoy a key competitive advantage: The huge mass of information they already have about their customers. The challenge is to turn that information into knowledge, and use the knowledge to give customers what they want.

It need hardly be said that the first thing customers want is better, quicker service on transparent terms and at an affordable price, in keeping with their own individual needs.

One of the implications is that customers should be able to interact fully with their bank, at any time and at any place, using their mobile devices. Today, there are 5 billion mobile phones in the world but only 1.2 billion bank customers. And mobile devices support an ever increasing range of functionalities. Mobile data traffic now stands at more than 2.5 exabytes per month, and will almost treble every two years.

This means on the one hand that the role of bank branches has radically changed; on the other, the potential scope of the banking market has widened immensely.

In the years to come the mobile phone will win a far greater share of interactions with banks. Technological progress—APIs [application program interfaces], cloud computing—and increased investment in mobile banking development (now standing at about $2 billion a year in terms of venture capital alone, plus the heavy internal investment of banks themselves) will lead to a powerful rise in the operational features of mobile devices and in the range and complexity of financial transactions they will support.

Nevertheless, many people still want to deal with their bank by other means: branch offices, ATMs, computers, conventional telephones, and an increasing number of "smart" devices. So banks need to offer their customers a genuinely "omnichannel" experience. The same value proposal, the same service, must be available at any time by any channel, and you should be able to switch from one channel to another instantly and seamlessly.

And of course customers will increasingly want their bank to offer content carrying higher value-added products and services that fit their needs more closely.

To meet these demands, banks must develop a new knowledge-based business model for the digital world.

According to Peter Weill, chair of the MIT [Massachusetts Institute of Technology] Sloan Center for Information Systems Research (CISR), the new digital model has three mainstays: first, content, the things being sold; secondly, customer experience—how the product or service is presented and used; and, thirdly, the technology platform, which shapes production and distribution.

I like to explain the construction of this new model by analogy to building a house. The technology platform is the foundation, while internal processes, organizational structures, and corporate culture are the various floors, including the installations (insulation, electricity, heating, plumbing, etc.). Finally, the channels by which customers interact with the bank are the roof of the house. All these elements together make the house comfortable and safe. They let us offer the customer a good product and a satisfying experience.

For many banks, the technology platform is a limiting factor and a nearly insurmountable challenge. Most bank platforms were designed and built in the 1960s and 70s. Professor Weill calls them "spaghetti platforms," because of the complexity of the connections resulting from several decades of add-ons, tweaks, and repairs.

This is why so many banks have tried to meet the digital challenge by building their "house" from the roof down, that is, starting with the channels. But that's a stopgap solution. Without strong foundations, the increased volume and sophistication of online banking will overburden the obsolete platforms and the house will ultimately collapse. . . .

Banks Must Embrace Big Data

Banks must take the lead in Big Data techniques if they are to make use of the competitive edge granted by their incumbent status. This can only be done with huge data-processing capabilities and a technological structure that fully and seamlessly

Attitudes Toward Banking with Non-Financial Institutions—North America

If these companies offered banking services, how likely would you be to bank with them?

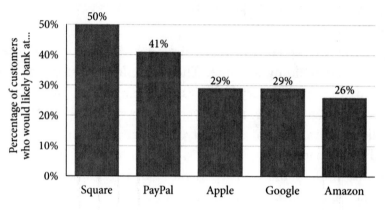

Source: Accenture, The Digital Disruption in Banking, 2014.

TAKEN FROM: John Heggestuen, "Emerging Start-Ups and Tech Giants Will Create New Winners and Losers in the Digital Banking Industry," Business Insider, October 22, 2014.

integrates the knowledge thus generated with every customer channel and every point of contact.

Such capabilities are still beyond the grasp of conventional banking platforms. Cloud computing, however, has created the possibility of enhancing them flexibly and efficiently. Many of the new entrants to the banking field will use cloud computing, and it can be an immensely useful tool for incumbent banks as well. But security concerns and regulatory and compliance requirements call for a very careful decision as to which data, transactions, and capabilities ought to remain on the bank's proprietary systems. The bank, what's more, must coordinate and integrate all cloud-based services. This highly complex task will be powerfully aided by a flexible and modern technology platform. . . .

Very few banks in the world have put themselves to the task with the necessary determination and depth. But our very survival is at stake. A new competitive landscape is taking shape in the financial services industry. A new ecosystem to which we must adapt.

Any number of these projects focus on transactions—payments, transfers, financial asset sales—such as PayPal, Dwolla, Square, M-Pesa, Billtrust, Kantox, Traxpay, etc. Adjoining this field we find companies that offer alternative currencies, such as Bitcoin, Bitstamp, Xapo, BitPay, etc.

Moving beyond the field of payments, initiatives are under way in other segments formerly monopolized by conventional banks: product and service selection advice (Bankrate, Money-SuperMarket, LendingTree, Credit Karma); personal finance management (Fintonic, Moven, Mint, etc.); investment and wealth management and advice (Betterment, Wealthfront, Sig-Fig, Personal Capital, Nutmeg); crowdfunding capital and debt financing (Lending Club, Kickstarter, Crowdfunder, AngelList, etc.). Lending to individuals—so far thought of as the segment most resistant to disintermediation—is being addressed by the preapproved loans industry (Lending Club, Prosper, Kreditech, Lenddo and many others).

Some companies are even trying to extract value from banking transaction data itself by providing customers with APIs to access their data, or directly supplying the tools for any business to manage its financial transactions on its own or for a bank to develop its digital offering (BancBox, Open Bank Project, Plaid, etc.).

The major online players (Google, Facebook, Amazon and Apple), leading telecoms companies and big retailers are taking a real interest in offering financial products to supplement their existing goods and services. There are several reasons for this. First, it enables them to offer their customers a fully rounded experience. Secondly, a financial relationship potentially entails multiple and recurring customer interactions through which a wealth of information can be extracted.

These players can supply a broader range of financial products and services and, eventually, create a full-fledged banking offer. At the very least they can create "packages" that combine their own products and services with financial products and services. These are packages that conventional banks will be hard-pressed to replicate.

We are witnessing the emergence of start-ups that focus on single segments of the value chain. These new entrants use the latest technology and lean, flexible structures to offer highly specific products. They can do so at cheap prices and offer a great customer experience by dint of speed, agility, and intensive use of Big Data technologies.

We are witnessing the disaggregation of the financial services industry, with a multitude of highly specialized competitors operating in different segments. What's more, major players are likely to enter the market with wider product ranges. So the banking industry—clearly burdened by overcapacity and in need of a far-reaching process of consolidation—will see an influx of competitors who will put still more pressure on incumbent banks' growth potential and bottom line.

Those banks that let the challenge of transformation go unmet, or fail in the attempt, are doomed to disappear.

> *"Low profitability and high regulations are legitimate deterrents for tech giants, and there absolutely is a big difference between becoming a bank and entering banking."*

Big Tech Does Not Pose a Serious Threat to Traditional Banks, but Could Change Banking

Jon Ogden

In the following viewpoint, Jon Ogden argues that while big tech's entry into the business of banking is sure to have a transformative effect on the banking industry, it will not be a serious threat to traditional banks. He contends that a number of key deterrents will keep tech giants from starting their own banks. At the same time, however, he does acknowledge that big tech's inevitable involvement in banking will absolutely change the way the banking industry works. Ogden is a contributor to Money Summit, a financial technology website.

As you read, consider the following questions:

1. According to Philippe Gellis, why won't tech giants enter the core business of banking?

Jon Ogden, "Tech Giants, P2P Lending, and How Banking Will Change Forever," Money Summit, August 14, 2014. Moneysummit.mx.com. Copyright © 2014 MX Technologies Inc. All rights reserved. Reproduced with permission.

2. According to Ogden, what function is at the core of retail banking?

3. Why are peer-to-peer lending companies a threat to traditional banks, according to the viewpoint?

The anxiety is building over whether a tech giant like Google, Amazon, or Facebook will enter the banking industry.

Just last week [in August 2014], two major articles on the topic surfaced—one from Philippe Gelis, CEO [chief executive officer] at Kantox, and one from Jim Marous, editor at the *Financial Brand*. Both articles received considerable attention on LinkedIn and Twitter.

Gelis asserts that the tech giants won't enter the core banking business of accepting deposits and originating loans because 1) they already have more profitable business models than banks do, 2) they despise the regulatory morass the banking industry is stuck in, and 3) they like to scale fast, and banking doesn't allow for that.

Marous agrees with Gelis that low profitability and high regulations are a hurdle to the tech giants, but he also draws a careful distinction between "becoming a bank" and "entering banking." He says that while it's true that tech giants have strong disincentives for officially becoming banks, they could enter banking at the edges—through the form of payment services, prepaid cards, merchant services, etc. Indeed, there's evidence with Google Wallet, Amazon Wallet, and Facebook Payments that these companies are already thinking this far ahead. They're starting to eat at the edges of banking.

Both of these articles present astute analyses on the banking industry. Low profitability and high regulations are legitimate deterrents for tech giants, and there absolutely is a big difference between becoming a bank and entering banking.

That said, there is one area that deserves additional attention when it comes to analyzing how the tech giants could enter the industry.

Peer-to-Peer Lending

At its core, retail banking is about connecting groups of people. Banks and credit unions are intermediaries that take deposit money and use it to offer loans at interest. That's the core of the business model—it rests on connecting people.

With the advent of the Internet, industries that connect people have changed forever. For example, Amazon altered the book industry, Airbnb changed the hotel industry, and Uber upended the taxi industry.

Here's what's going on, in the simplest terms:

- Amazon connects people who want a book to people who need a book.

- Airbnb connects people who have a room to people who need a room.

- Uber connects people who have a car to people who need a car ride.

It's all about connecting people. The moment it was possible for someone in Tennessee to order a book from Seattle and get it shipped to them for cheap, the need for a physical bookstore in Tennessee started to diminish. Likewise, once it was possible for riders to connect to a driver via phone, the need for a traditional taxicab started to fade. By making global connection easy, the Internet is eliminating traditional methods of intermediation.

Banks and credit unions should take note.

This week *Harvard Business Review* wrote a piece on the rise of lending technologies. It says that these technologies—powered by companies like Prosper, Square Capital, Funding Circle, Lending Club, and Fundera—have already started to eat into the small business and personal loan market.

So here's what's crucial for banks and credit unions to consider: These lending companies are connecting people who want to invest with people who want a loan, and that alone means that traditional intermediaries are in trouble.

Right now, peer-to-peer lending is insignificant in the grand scheme, but what happens when a tech giant acquires one of these companies? And the tech giant doesn't necessarily have to be Google, Amazon, or Facebook. It could be one of the major US banks (which are becoming tech giants in their own right), it could be Walmart, or it could be someone totally new to the scene. In fact, it could even be a forward-looking community bank or credit union.

However it happens, the very fact that peer-to-peer lending technology exists and is already being used signifies that the core of the banking industry will likely be upended—just like the core of other industries has been. . . .

If I'm a Mint user, I could already be bypassing my bank or credit union to get a small business loan or an auto loan. That should wake financial institutions up to the fact that Mint is a major competitor to them, and it should wake the bigger banks up to idea that peer-to-peer lending could eventually expand to include larger loans.

It's really not outside the realm of possibility for peer-to-peer lending to eventually become the norm. I mean, if I'm from Tennessee and I'm looking for a good rate on a loan, why do I care what state the money comes from? If a company like Lending Club can get investors from Seattle or Maine or Texas and offer a better rate, I'll be tempted to take the offer. And once Lending Club grows bigger or gets acquired by a tech giant it will become an instant threat to the traditional banking business model.

The Future

Of course, the concerns that Philippe Gelis and Jim Marous brought up in their articles still hold sway. Profitability is low and regulations are high. Peer-to-peer lenders will likely soon enough find themselves wading through regulatory sludge and they will discover, if they haven't already, just how difficult it is to enter banking. But the fact that the technology exists means that banking, like almost every other industry, will never be the same. Banks and credit unions can either adopt these new technologies or find themselves irrelevant soon enough. At this point, it's only a matter of time before banking changes forever.

*"Project Loon has the potential to greatly
change how 60% of the world lives."*

Project Loon
Is a Potentially Great
Technological Breakthrough

Angela Washeck

*In the following viewpoint, Angela Washeck argues that Google's
Project Loon is an extremely important initiative with significant
global implications. She contends that the project, which aims to
bring Internet service to some of the most remote regions of the
planet via floating Wi-Fi balloons, has the potential to change
life for the better for an untold number of underserved people
worldwide. Washeck is a writer and an English teacher who
regularly contributes to* Paste *magazine and other publications.*

As you read, consider the following questions:

1. According to Washeck, what percentage of those who
   currently lack Internet service will get service through
   Project Loon?

2. Where will Project Loon balloons be found, and how
   will they move, according to the viewpoint?

3. According to Washeck, how will Project Loon balloons be powered?

Google has a lot of interesting and groundbreaking projects in the pipeline—driverless cars, Google Glass, Google Fiber, and even the ones that spawn from their creepy obsession with human immortality. Many of these come from a mysterious branch of the company known as Google X and probably will never see the light of day. However, Project Loon just might be the most important project going on over in Mountain View, [California, where Google headquarters are located].

What Is Project Loon?

Project Loon's tagline is "balloon-powered Internet for everyone"—and when they say everyone, they really mean everyone. As noted in the video, Google's aim with Project Loon is to deliver high-speed Internet to the estimated 60% of the world's population who don't currently have access to it. But according to Google, they don't just want a bunch of new Google+ users—they believe in the power that the Internet brings to those who don't have access to things like medical information, higher education, and worldwide communication.

Project Loon is fittingly dubbed because it enlists balloons to deliver Internet access to the world's most remote areas. It seeks to level the digital playing field, particularly to make information available affordably to areas of the world without the ability to seek medical knowledge, establish local businesses online and pursue online education. But how? These balloons are a special technology that floats up in the stratosphere, twice as high as airplanes fly. "Loon balloons" get around with the aid of the wind, which really thrives in the stratosphere.

These different directions and speeds of wind guide the balloons, whether up or down, and people down below can connect to a balloon network through a special Internet antenna attached to whatever structure they're in (home, workplace, coffee shop). "The signal bounces from this antenna up to the balloon network, and then down to the global Internet on Earth," according to Google Loon's official website.

That's great and all, but is it fast Internet? Google says that each balloon, which can float for about 100 days in the stratosphere, is capable of establishing an Internet connection "to a ground area about 40 km in diameter at speeds comparable to 3G." Apparently, the balloons can communicate with each other and on-the-ground Google folks with their installed radio antennas. These balloons look remarkably like actual balloons, Google says, because their electronic functions are all stored in one box underneath the inflated part—almost like the basket you would see on a hot air balloon.

What's more, the Loon balloons seem to be a much more environmentally friendly way of getting Internet access out to people. Outfitted with solar panels, which produce 100 watts of power in full sun, the balloons run on solar power during the day and a battery at night.

PCWorld says Google may be hanging out in the Nevada desert with Loon balloons these days. After an initial trial in New Zealand, Martyn Williams reported that Google was looking to tap into LTE [long-term evolution] technology with the approval of the FCC [Federal Communications Commission]. This is significant because the tests, which are apparently being done in northern Nevada, fall in "two chunks of radio spectrum that are used as a pair for 4G LTE services," Williams wrote. What's clear is that the tests are a secret. "The technology is under development and highly sensitive and confidential in nature," Google wrote to the FCC. "The release of such information would provide valuable insight into Google's technology innovations and potential business plans and strategies."

What Project Loon Aims to Do

Mike Cassidy, Project Loon's leader, says the technology is now sufficiently cheap and reliable for Google to start planning how to roll it out. By the end of 2015, he wants to have enough balloons in the air to test nearly continuous service in several parts of the Southern Hemisphere. Commercial deployment would follow: Google expects cellular providers to rent access to the balloons to expand their networks. Then the number of people in the world who still lack Internet access should start to shrink, fast.

Tom Simonite, "Project Loon,"
MIT Technology Review, *February 18, 2015.*

Google, Facebook, and Spreading the Internet's Reach

But Google isn't just sitting on their hands with Project Loon. On April 14 [2014], Google extended the shelf life of this dream by acquiring a drone start-up company called Titan Aerospace. As with every bizarre Google acquisition of late, a couple of important questions need to be asked: What do they do and what does Google want from them?

Titan Aerospace is an innovative company—an understandable fit for Google, always looking for ways to stay a step ahead of its competitors. Titan Aerospace uses its high-altitude drone technologies to "help people," they say, both through providing web connections and "monitoring environmental damage like oil spills and deforestation." According to Tech-Crunch, Google plans to use the research, data, and expertise from the folks working with Titan drones, which reportedly fly up to 65,000 feet for up to three years, to help make up for the two-thirds of the globe's population without Internet access.

In doing so, Google is partnering with people who know about the risks, costs and opportunities of dealing with unmanned aerial objects. According to the writer from Tech-Crunch, "The use of drones could conceivably make a network of Internet-providing automatons even better at globetrotting, with a higher degree of control and ability to react to changing conditions. Some kind of hybrid system might also be in the pipeline that marries both technologies." However, Google wasn't the only company interested in Titan Aerospace.

TechCrunch also reported in March that Facebook was expressing some serious interest in acquiring Titan Aerospace for about $60 million, but then Mark Zuckerberg and company announced their purchase of UK-based Ascenta for an undisclosed amount. The drone maker is helping sponsor Facebook's new Connectivity Lab, which Zuckerberg said they would use to beam the World Wide Web to low-income countries through air and space technologies.

The Connectivity Lab is part of the bigger Internet.org project, hoping to bring Internet to 5 billion people. Whether its advertising dollars or new ventures, Facebook and Google are constantly competing. Now, their aerial projects (Project Loon and Connectivity Lab) may make the competition a bit more interesting. It's easy to look at what Facebook and Google are doing through Internet.org and see nothing but greedy capitalism at work. After all, Google wants nothing more than to gain more customers of the products, more users of their services, and ultimately more eyeballs for advertisers.

But unlike Google's other initiatives, whether it's a nice new Nexus smartphone or the next big thing in wearable technology, Project Loon has the potential to greatly change how 60% of the world lives. These are the kinds of changes that have a positive effect that may never fully be able to be calculated—that is, if Google can really do what they say they can. Either way, at this point it's hard not to cheer them on.

> "With every fiber of my being I want Project Loon to succeed . . . but part of me . . . believes that Google's Project Loon's evangelists were perhaps a bit too idealistic in their high school model UN classes."

Project Loon Is Unlikely to Succeed

Kevin Fitchard

In the following viewpoint, Kevin Fitchard argues that Google's Project Loon idea, while noble, is probably doomed to failure. He contends that Google has seriously underestimated the political implications of Project Loon and the degree of backlash it is likely to receive from hostile governments uninterested in allowing their citizens to have unfettered Internet access. In short, he believes that even with the best intentions, the political issues that Project Loon will encounter will eventually ground the ambitious project. Fitchard is a technology writer and reporter with a specialty in wireless networks.

As you read, consider the following questions:

1. According to Fitchard, why will Project Loon's use of spectrum be a problem?

2. How will Project Loon's balloons be different from the satellites created by Iridium and Globalstar, according to the viewpoint?

3. According to Jillian York, how might Project Loon's balloons be threatened by volatile governments?

The balloon-powered network known as [Project] Loon may be one of Google's famed moon shots, but the biggest issues facing the project are grounded right here on Earth. This won't just be a major technological feat for Google. It will be a huge political undertaking. I give Google credit: It's never shied away from a challenge. But if Loon is going to be a success, it's going to have to wade deeply into the morass of global international relations.

I say this because Loon is no ordinary network—and I'm not referring to the balloons. Google wants to build a network that knows no borders. Not only does Google want to implement it in every country with an underserved Internet population, but the network itself will be stateless, coasting from continent to continent.

Loon would basically become an Internet service provider above the clouds. Terrestrial radios on the ground would link to solar-powered balloons floating 12 miles up in the stratosphere. These balloons would link to each other to form a mesh network, bouncing signals off one another until they reach a ground-based station with a fiber connection to the Internet. Google will have some control over where these balloons go by navigating the wind currents, but as Google shows in its Loon videos, its eventual plan is to set them loose in the sky, letting them follow the west-east stratospheric winds around the world.

"If the balloons are circling over the bottom half of the world, eventually the balloon that's over South Africa will pass over South America," Google captain of moon shots Astro Teller explained in one such video.

Well, Iran happens to be at the same latitude as Texas. The same network infrastructure floating over the U.S. will make its way above Middle Eastern countries with which the U.S. isn't exactly on the best terms. *I'm* not saying that's a bad thing. The Internet should transcend international boundaries, and it does more to help international relations than it does harm. But I doubt every world leader will see that way.

Since Loon will use radios, it will have to use spectrum, which is tightly regulated by the world's governments. It can't just use any old spectrum either. It will have to convince hundreds of different regulators to agree on a unified band or ride over an existing one—such as the unlicensed airwaves used for Wi-Fi. But the scope and range of Google's Loon network will likely require dedicated airwaves. Just imagine a Wi-Fi network blasting down at high power from the heavens. If your wireless router is using the same airwaves, it will be drowned out.

And we're not talking about a scenario as simple as Wi-Fi, where airwaves are ultimately shared by multiple entities. We're talking about Google becoming a global ISP [Internet service provider], actually providing or selling Internet service. ISPs, like any communications service provider, are regulated, and governments will likely want some say in how that access is offered, what Google can charge, and ultimately whom Google is allowed to connect.

Go, Go Google

I'm sure Google has weighed all of these potential obstacles, and that makes its willingness to push ahead all the more admirable and daring (or all the more crazy, depending on how you look at it).

I'm certainly not saying Google can't accomplish its goal. Google has dealt plenty with regulators and governments in the past, and it has already cut its teeth in the international spectrum arena by working with governments on white space broadband.

The Lunacy of Project Loon

The project's name makes it seem inoffensive, unobjectionable. But the longer you look at the [Project] Loon craft, the less they look like balloons. If Google's claims about the Loon balloons' navigability are true, it is in fact an 'unmanned aircraft,' sometimes more pejoratively referred to as a drone. And what's worrisome is not so much Google's stated goal, but that with unprecedented proprietary technology, scant law on the books, and a few key government connections, Project Loon may only be a harbinger of a new era in our relationship to the skies overhead, one that our laws are dramatically unprepared for.

Will Butler, "Can We Trust Google with the Stratosphere?,"
Atlantic, August 20, 2013.

There's also a precedent for truly global communications providers, namely the satellite networks that traverse the heavens. Loon is very similar to the low Earth orbit satellite constellations built by Iridium and Globalstar and uses the same mesh-networking principles. Those birds zip over the globe just above the atmosphere and ignore international borders. The main difference is that Google's balloons are surfing the atmospheric wind currents, while Iridium and Globalstar are riding Earth's gravitational pull.

But space is still an open frontier, loosely regulated by international treaties. Most governments consider the stratosphere above them their sovereign airspace, which is why they shoot down spy planes that venture into it.

Earlier today [in June 2013], I participated in a panel discussion about the feasibility of Loon on HuffPost Live, in which the Electronic Frontier Foundation's Jillian York raised a telling question: How long before some unstable government seeking to wreak havoc on its world's communications infrastructure starts shooting down Loon balloons overhead?

A United Nations (UN) of Broadband

Google might opt to keep the network limited. It has some control of the movements of the balloons. It can increase or decrease their altitude, catching cross currents. It could feasibly keep the Loon gird centered over specific countries by letting the balloons track back and forth. But Google's ultimate goal seems to be to let them float free, blanketing the world in constantly shifting floating mesh.

Loon is truly a noble project, and, sure, Google has profit motive in connecting billions more people to the Internet. But this is how technology and communications revolutions are born—one company with a crazy idea for a network and the wherewithal and resources to implement it.

Technology isn't a barrier. Mesh networks are nothing new, and dirigibles have been around since the time of *Graf Zeppelin* [a German airship in operation in the mid-twentieth century]. The minefield here is entirely political. With every fiber of my being I want Project Loon to succeed, and I'm actually fairly in awe of Google for having the chutzpah to attempt it. But part of me also believes that Google's Project Loon's evangelists were perhaps a bit too idealistic in their high school model UN classes.

> *"I have no idea what an Apple Car would look like or how it would work. But Apple has a proven track record of astounding people by reinventing ordinary products. . . . It wouldn't put its energy into a car unless Apple thought it could make something special."*

A Car Designed by Apple Is a Realistic Possibility

Michelle Quinn

In the following viewpoint, Michelle Quinn argues that the idea of Apple building its own car is not so far-fetched. She contends that it makes sense for Apple to enter the automotive market and that such an endeavor would only add to the company's already powerful reach among consumers. If Apple did not pursue a branded car, she suggests, the company would risk its reputation as a leader in the tech industry, especially as other tech giants are already planning and manufacturing their own branded vehicles. Quinn is a contributing writer who covers Silicon Valley and technology news for the San Jose Mercury News.

As you read, consider the following questions:

1. According to Quinn, what is "the third space"?

2. How would producing a car allow Apple to answer its detractors' criticisms, according to Quinn?

3. According to the viewpoint, why would Apple have a particular advantage in designing its own car in regard to its unique customer base?

Think about all the reasons that it is a bad idea. For one thing, the auto industry isn't for the faint of heart. It is tough to make money, and the industry regularly grapples with complex safety, labor and regulatory issues around the globe. As Exhibit A, look at the recall of faulty air bags taking place right now [in February 2015].

In addition, the field is crowded with scrappy worldwide and U.S. competition—and that's before the Chinese have made a big push in the car market.

If it is serious, Apple may also be a little late to the game, since Tesla [Motors] has already captured much of the excitement over beautiful, high-performing electric cars, and Google is well along in its efforts to bring the future closer with self-driving cars.

It's also hard to imagine Apple designers wanting to craft state-of-the-art cup holders, bumpers and seat belts. In an interview with Bloomberg News, Dan Akerson, the former CEO [chief executive officer] of General Motors, described Apple making a car as "trying to cough up a hairball."

But people are focusing on trivial concerns and overlooking what is at stake for Apple. The iPhone maker could remake the automobile, and the car could reinvent Apple.

Moving into the Automotive Market

Cars have long been known as "the third space," the place where we spend a large chunk of time outside of home and work. In our cars, we are a very captive audience.

The car is the "ultimate mobile device," said Thilo Koslowski, a vice president and the automotive practice leader at Gartner. But today the car is the least "smart" device out there, he added.

Enter Apple, which needs to worry about its next big area of growth. To find it, the company has to become an even bigger part of consumers' lives, which are already saturated with iPhones and iPads.

We still spend a lot on cars. Outside of buying a home, purchasing a car is the biggest expense for most consumers. And the industry is growing, said Karl Brauer, a senior analyst with Kelley Blue Book.

Apple has "the financial and intellectual engineering might to become a car manufacturer if they want to," Brauer said. "The big challenge is, would they be satisfied only making 5 to 10 percent profit? You can find a lot more reasons not to be a car manufacturer than to be one. But then again, no one would have thought of investing in digital music players, and that reinvented the company."

An Apple Car?

Already, Apple has a dashboard system called CarPlay (Google has a similar system called Android Auto) that is sold in some cars. It offers buttons to do things such as send a text hands free or to make a call.

But CarPlay is just the beginning, analysts say. The more ambitious idea would be for Apple to curate the car experience, from controlling the aesthetics to bridging the digital divide between the vehicle and the smartphone.

That sounds interesting, but I can't imagine Apple happy with being the user interface provider to General Motors or Ford, even if the automakers make co-branded "Apple cars," similar to what PC [personal computer] makers did with Intel with its "Intel Inside" campaign.

Apple may feel the need to be bolder. One knock on the company is that even with its nearly $200 billion in the bank and quarter after quarter of record sales, it doesn't take advantage of its creativity and know-how to do more. Its newest product, Apple Watch, which goes on sale in April, is exciting but not a world changer. It's more like a cool iPhone accessory.

An Apple Car would answer that critique and transform the company.

It would be a tremendous leap, given the company's focus on "extreme quality control," said Alan Deutschman, author of *The Second Coming of Steve Jobs* and a business journalism professor at the University of Nevada, Reno. He is skeptical about the Apple Car. But still, "when you are a company sitting on a tremendous amount of cash, there is this pressure to invest in the next big thing. There's a temptation to say, 'We're the smartest around. Let's attempt it.'"

And finally, the Apple Car makes sense because there will be a market among the Apple fans who, rather than hold an Apple device, would want to be inside one.

I have no idea what an Apple Car would look like or how it would work.

But Apple has a proven track record of astounding people by reinventing ordinary products such as the music player, the phone and the watch. It wouldn't put its energy into a car unless Apple thought it could make something special.

Periodical and Internet Sources Bibliography

The following articles have been selected to supplement the diverse views presented in this chapter.

Jon Brodkin	"Google Balloons, 'Cell Towers in the Sky,' Can Serve 4G to a Whole State," Ars Technica, March 11, 2015.
Will Butler	"Can We Trust Google with the Stratosphere?," *Atlantic*, August 20, 2013.
Chris Ciaccia	"Apple Car Is Definitely Coming—Just Ask Carl Icahn," The Street, May 18, 2015.
John Gapper	"Technology Will Hurt the Banks, Not Kill Them," *Financial Times*, October 15, 2014.
Philippe Gelis	"Why Tech Giants (Google, Apple, Amazon, Facebook . . .) Will Probably Never Become Banks!," LinkedIn, August 5, 2014.
Adam Hayes	"Technology, the Biggest Threat for Big Banks," Investopedia, April 1, 2015.
Anna Irrera	"Tech Giants Threaten Existence of Retail Banks," *Financial News*, April 30, 2015.
Erika Morphy	"Not to Be a Buzzkill, but an Apple Car Will Kill Privacy," *Forbes*, May 30, 2015.
Doug Newcomb	"Why an Apple Car Makes Sense," *PC Magazine*, February 20, 2015.
Will Oremus	"Not as Loony as It Sounds," *Slate*, December 2, 2014.
Don Reisinger	"Apple Car a Possibility—Just Not Anytime Soon," CNET, April 14, 2015.

For Further Discussion

Chapter 1

1. Lyndsey Gilpin argues that tech giants are socially responsible, while Gabriel Thompson argues that they are socially irresponsible. With which author do you agree more, and why?

2. Monika Bauerlein and Clara Jeffery and Harry Bruinius take opposite sides in the argument over whether tech giants are taking a stand against government surveillance or playing an active role in perpetuating it. In your opinion, do Bauerlein and Jeffery or does Bruinius make a better case? Explain your reasoning.

3. Adam Hudson contends that tech giants such as Google are causing extreme gentrification in urban areas. Do you agree with his viewpoint, or do you think that tech giants are having a positive effect on urban neighborhoods, as Mackenzie Carpenter and Deborah M. Todd argue? Explain your reasoning, citing text from the viewpoints to support your answer.

4. Tate Williams and David Pomerantz offer different opinions on the environmental friendliness of big tech companies. Do you think tech giants are doing a good job of being environmentally conscious? Why, or why not?

Chapter 2

1. Brian Proffitt asserts that Google Glass poses a serious threat to personal privacy. Do you believe he presents enough evidence to support this argument? Explain your answer. What is your opinion of the Google Glass technology? Explain.

2. Ted Samson argues that cloud computing services are dangerously insecure and prone to breaches. Do you agree with his opinion? Why, or why not?

3. Sam Mattera and James Kendrick take opposite sides in the debate over whether the high prices Apple charges for its products are justified. With whom do you agree more? Why?

4. Christa Avampato argues in favor of tech giants such as Amazon using drones to deliver packages. Do you think delivery drones are a good idea? Why, or why not? Cite at least two pros and two cons that you can think of concerning drone delivery systems.

Chapter 3

1. Wade Roush argues that Google is a monopoly, while Ryan Radia asserts that it is not. In your opinion, is Google a monopoly? Why, or why not? Cite text from the viewpoints to support your answer.

2. Robert Hatta contends that acqui-hires stifle innovation and are ultimately harmful to the tech industry. Do you agree with his opinion? Why, or why not?

3. Jamie Salvatori argues that third-party online retailers such as Amazon and eBay are harmful to small businesses. In your opinion, are online retailers beneficial or detrimental to small businesses? Explain your reasoning.

Chapter 4

1. Francisco González and Jon Ogden offer different opinions on whether tech giants pose a serious threat to traditional banks. Do you think tech giants will take over the banking industry in the future? Why, or why not? If tech giants do become involved in banking, do you think it will be a positive or negative outcome? Explain your reasoning.

2. Angela Washeck argues that Google's Project Loon is an important humanitarian effort that is sure to succeed, while Kevin Fitchard says it is probably doomed to fail. With which author do you agree more? Explain your answer. What do you think is the biggest obstacle standing in the way of Project Loon's success? Explain.

3. After reading the viewpoint by Michelle Quinn, do you think tech giants such as Apple or Google should become involved in other markets such as automobiles, or should they concentrate on computers, tablets, smartphones, etc.? Do you think the computer industry and automobile industry are connected in some way? Explain your reasoning.

Organizations to Contact

The editors have compiled the following list of organizations concerned with the issues debated in this book. The descriptions are derived from materials provided by the organizations. All have publications or information available for interested readers. The list was compiled on the date of publication of the present volume; the information provided here may change. Be aware that many organizations take several weeks or longer to respond to inquiries, so allow as much time as possible.

Berkman Center for Internet & Society
23 Everett Street, 2nd Floor, Cambridge, MA   02138
(617) 495-7547 • fax: (617) 495-7641
e-mail: cyber@law.harvard.edu
website: http://cyber.law.harvard.edu

The Berkman Center for Internet & Society is a cyberspace research center that focuses on legal, technical, and social issues tied to the online world and assesses the need for new Internet laws and sanctions. The center publishes a variety of podcasts, blog posts, and articles related to its research efforts. Many of these publications are available on its website, including its annual reports, blog posts such as "Radio Berkman 179: The Googleplex," and interactive multimedia exhibits including "Brad Smith and Jonathan Zittrain on Privacy, Surveillance, and Rebuilding Trust in Tech."

Center for Democracy & Technology (CDT)
1634 I Street NW #1100, Washington, DC   20006
(202) 637-9800 • fax: (202) 637-0968
website: www.cdt.org

The Center for Democracy & Technology (CDT) is an online civil liberties advocacy group that seeks to ensure that regulations related to current and emerging forms of technology align with America's democratic values, particularly those of free expression and privacy. To promote its ideology, the CDT engages in research and education projects, grassroots movements, and more. On its website, the CDT posts articles, reports, and other publications, including "Testimony—'Drones: The Next Generation of Commerce?'" and "Apple Ups the Encryption Ante: Don't Get Left Behind."

Electronic Frontier Foundation (EFF)

815 Eddy Street, San Francisco, CA 94109
(415) 436-9333 • fax: (415) 436-9993
e-mail: info@eff.org
website: www.eff.org

The Electronic Frontier Foundation (EFF) is an organization that seeks to raise the public's awareness of telecommunications issues. It works to bring attention to the myriad civil liberties issues that arise as the result of advancements in computer-based communications and pursues litigation necessary to preserve, defend, and extend First Amendment rights in computer and telecom technologies. EFF's publications include the biweekly electronic newsletter *EFFector Online*, white papers, articles, and blog posts, including "Eight Tech Giants Call for Reform to Surveillance Laws" and "Global Network Initiative Gets an Inside Look at Tech Firms' Human Rights Practices."

Federal Trade Commission (FTC)

600 Pennsylvania Avenue NW, Washington, DC 20580
(202) 326-2222
website: www.ftc.gov

The Federal Trade Commission (FTC) is a government agency tasked with overseeing the various issues of everyday economic life. The FTC's primary aim is to protect consumers from deceptive or anticompetitive business practices and ensure that commerce occurs fairly and within the legal boundaries established by federal and state legislatures and US and global government agencies. As part of its efforts, the FTC publishes a broad range of reports, policy statements, advisory opinions, studies, and many other documents that are available on its website.

Institute for Ethics & Emerging Technologies (IEET)

56 Daleville School Road, Willington, CT   06279
(860) 428-1837
website: www.ieet.org

Founded in 2004, the Institute for Ethics & Emerging Technologies (IEET) is a nonprofit think tank that promotes ideas about how technological progress can increase freedom and human advancement in democratic societies. Focusing on emerging technologies that have the potential to positively transform social conditions and the quality of human lives, IEET seeks to cultivate understanding of their implications and encourage responsible public policies for their safe use. IEET publishes the *Journal of Evolution and Technology*, and its website features the *Ethical Technology* blog as well as articles, books, and white papers.

Internet Association

1100 H Street NW, Suite 1020, Washington, DC   20005
e-mail: contact@internetassociation.org
website: internetassociation.org

The Internet Association is a coalition of major online businesses that works to advance policy solutions that protect Internet freedoms, encourage continued innovation and economic advancement, and give users a voice in the Internet's development. Among the high-profile businesses that make up the Internet Association are tech giants such as Amazon, Facebook, Google, Netflix, Twitter, and PayPal. Its blog features links to articles such as "Washington's 100 Top Tech Leaders" and "Stand Up for Your Rights: U.S. Senate to Move on Government Surveillance Reform."

Internet Society

1775 Wiehle Avenue, Suite 201, Reston, VA 20190-5108

(703) 439-2120 • fax: (703) 326-9881

e-mail: isoc@isoc.org

website: www.internetsociety.org

The Internet Society is a global organization that works to ensure that the Internet will continue to develop as an empowering open platform for the exchange of ideas. Founded in 1992, the Internet Society specializes in three main areas: standards, public policy, and education. Supported by more than sixty-five thousand members in more than one hundred chapters worldwide, the Internet Society seeks to facilitate change through the application of its collective technological and communications expertise. As part of its efforts, the Internet Society produces an array of publications, including reports such as "History of the Internet Holds the Keys to Its Future" and "Does a Digital Society Have to Become a Surveillance Society?"

National Telecommunications & Information Administration (NTIA)

Herbert C. Hoover Building (HCHB)

US Department of Commerce

National Telecommunications and
    Information Administration

Washington, DC 20230

(703) 292-5111

website: www.ntia.doc.go

The National Telecommunications & Information Administration (NTIA) is an executive branch government agency that is responsible for advising the president on policy issues related to telecommunications and information. Outside of that responsibility, NTIA sponsors a variety of programs aimed at expanding broadband Internet access and ensuring that the Internet remains a free and open medium for innovation and the exchange of ideas. In the course of its operations, NTIA produces numerous publications, including reports such as "Broadband Availability in the Workplace" and "Exploring the Digital Nation: America's Emerging Online Experience."

Pew Research Center
1615 L Street NW, Suite 800, Washington, DC   20036
(202) 419-4300 • fax: (202) 419-4349
website: www.pewinternet.org

The Pew Research Center is a nonpartisan think tank that examines the various issues and trends that impact modern American society. Pew's Internet, Science and Tech project focuses on the impact of the Internet on children, family life, communities, business, education, health care, and other facets of daily life. On its website, the Internet, Science and Tech project publishes a vast array of articles, presentations, and reports, including "The Changing Privacy Landscape" and "The Fourth Digital Revolution."

Union of Concerned Scientists (UCS)
2 Brattle Square, Cambridge, MA   02138-3780
(617) 547-5552 • fax: (617) 864-9405
website: www.ucsusa.org

Founded in 1969 by the Massachusetts Institute of Technology (MIT) faculty and students, the Union of Concerned Scientists (UCS) is an activist organization focused on studying the effects science and technology innovations have on the environment and seeking out better practical solutions when necessary. UCS aims to use technical analysis and effective advocacy to create innovative, practical solutions for a healthy, safe, and sustainable future. Its publications include *Catalyst*, the official UCS magazine, and *Earthwise*, its quarterly member newsletter. Its website features *The Equation* blog with articles such as "How Green Is Your Data? Tech Companies and Energy Use" and "Google and the EPA's Clean Power Plan: Leaders and Fortune 500 Companies Unite in Support of Renewable Energy."

Bibliography of Books

Charles Arthur *Digital Wars: Apple, Google, Microsoft and the Battle for the Internet.* Philadelphia, PA: Kogan Page Ltd., 2012.

George Beahm *The Google Boys: Sergey Brin and Larry Page in Their Own Words.* Evanston, IL: B2 Books, 2014.

Nick Bilton *Hatching Twitter: A True Story of Money, Power, Friendship, and Betrayal.* London: Hodder & Stoughton, 2013.

Eric Butow and Robert Stepisnik *Google Glass for Dummies.* Hoboken, NJ: John Wiley & Sons Inc., 2014.

Nicholas Carlson *Marissa Mayer and the Fight to Save Yahoo!* New York: Twelve, 2015.

Luke Dormehl *The Apple Revolution: Steve Jobs, the Counter Culture and How the Crazy Ones Took Over the World.* London: Virgin Books, 2012.

Brad Durant *Google Glass: The Ultimate Guide for Understanding Google Glass and What You Need to Know.* Seattle, WA: CreateSpace, 2014.

Andrew V. Edwards *Digital Is Destroying Everything: What the Tech Giants Won't Tell You About How Robots, Big Data, and Algorithms Are Radically Remaking Your Future.* Lanham, MD: Rowman & Littlefield, 2015.

Ken Hillis, Michael Petit, and Kylie Jarrett   *Google and the Culture of Search.* New York: Routledge, 2013.

Walter Isaacson   *The Innovators: How a Group of Hackers, Geniuses, and Geeks Created the Digital Revolution.* New York: Simon & Schuster, 2014.

Leander Kahney   *Jony Ive: The Genius Behind Apple's Greatest Products.* New York: Portfolio/Penguin, 2013.

Adam Lashinsky   *Inside Apple: How America's Most Admired—and Secretive—Company Really Works.* London: John Murray Publishers, 2012.

Michael S. Malone   *The Intel Trinity: How Robert Noyce, Gordon Moore, and Andy Grove Built the World's Most Important Company.* New York: HarperCollins, 2014.

Gayle Laakmann McDowell   *Cracking the Tech Career: Insider Advice on Landing a Job at Google, Microsoft, Apple, or Any Top Tech Company.* Hoboken, NJ: John Wiley & Sons Inc., 2014.

Jacquie McNish and Sean Silcoff   *Losing the Signal: The Untold Story Behind the Extraordinary Rise and Spectacular Fall of BlackBerry.* New York: Flatiron Books, 2015.

Deborah Perry Piscione   *Secrets of Silicon Valley: What Everyone Else Can Learn from the Innovation Capital of the World.* New York: Palgrave Macmillan, 2013.

Arun Rao   *A History of Silicon Valley: The Greatest Creation of Wealth in the History of the Planet.* 2nd ed. Palo Alto, CA: Omniware Group, 2013.

John Rossman   *The Amazon Way: 14 Leadership Principles Behind the World's Most Disruptive Company.* Seattle, WA: CreateSpace, 2014.

Brent Schlender and Rick Tetzeli   *Becoming Steve Jobs: The Evolution of a Reckless Upstart into a Visionary Leader.* New York: Crown Business, 2015.

Eric Schmidt and Jonathan Rosenberg   *How Google Works.* New York: Grand Central Publishing, 2014.

Timothy Sprinkle   *Screw the Valley: A Coast-to-Coast Tour of America's New Tech Startup Culture.* Dallas, TX: BenBella Books Inc., 2015.

Brad Stone   *The Everything Store: Jeff Bezos and the Age of Amazon.* New York: Back Bay Books, 2014.

Ashlee Vance   *Elon Musk: Tesla, Space X, and the Quest for a Fantastic Future.* New York: HarperCollins, 2015.

Fred Vogelstein   *Dogfight: How Apple and Google Went to War and Started a Revolution.* New York: Sarah Crichton Books, 2013.

Index

A

Access to the Internet
  new markets, 45, 202
  political barriers, 204, 207–208
  Project Loon, 182, 198–203, 204–208
Acer, 125*t*
"Acqui-hiring," 145–146, 167, 168, 172, 173
  hires will become innovators, 165–170
  innovation stifled, 146, 151–154, 171–175
Activism. *See* Community activism
Adams, David, 160
AdMob, 152, 169
AdWords, 151, 153
Affordable Housing Network, 39
African Americans, San Francisco and Bay area, 69–70, 72, 77–78
Aguirre, Robert, 39
Air disasters, 139, 140, 141
Air pollution, 28, 87
Air Pollution Control Act (1955), 28
Airbnb, 195
Akerson, Dan, 210
Alkali Act (UK; 1863), 27
Aloise, Rome, 37
Amazon, 195
  cloud services, 117–118, 119
  data centers, 25, 87–88
  delivery drones are a bad idea, 137, 138–142

  delivery drones are a good idea, 131, 132, 135–136
  energy sources, and environmental harms, 22–23, 23–24, 25, 26, 30, 85, 86–89
  financial industry services, 190*t*, 191–192, 194
  food delivery systems, 132–133
  tablets, 124, 125*t*
  third-party retailers' effects on small business, 145, 176, 177–179
American Electric Power, 88–89
American Legislative Exchange Council (ALEC), 25
Android, 149, 152
  market share, 123–124
  tablets, 124–125, 125*t*
  See also Google
Anti-competitive businesses. *See* Monopolies
Anti-Eviction Mapping Project, 69
Antitrust investigations, 157, 161
Antitrust laws, 162, 163
Apple
  acqui-hiring, 167
  cars, 183, 209–213
  environmental policy, 29, 80, 81–84, 167
  financial industry services, 190*t*, 191–192
  history, 15, 151
  iCloud, 83, 112–113, 114, 117–118
  internal security breaches, 112–113, 114
  iPad, 123, 124–125, 125*t*, 126

Energy Information Administration reports, 22, 24
Energy use
drones, 140
Internet power, 21–23, 23–24, 25, 26, 33, 83, 85, 86–89
See also Renewable energy use
Environmental movement, 27–28
Environmental Protection Agency (EPA)
energy rulings, 24
staff, 81
Environmentalism
companies can be environmentally friendly, 80–84
companies can be environmentally harmful, 85–89
companies' social responsibility, 18, 20, 21–33, 86–89
reports and ratings, 22, 81, 82, 83
Evictions, 65–66, 67–68, 69, 70, 73–74

F

Facebook
acqui-hiring, 166, 168–169, 170, 172
acquisitions, 168, 202
business model, 48, 49, 168, 169–170
Connectivity Lab, 202
facial recognition technology, 93
financial industry services, 182, 191–192, 194
location, 35–36
NSA surveillance and response, 42, 44, 50–51
NSA surveillance and role, 47, 48–49, 50

renewable energy power and policy, 22, 31, 86, 88
service industry workers, 37
targeted advertising, 48
Facial recognition technology
Facebook, 93
Google, 98–99, 103, 107–108
implications, 98–99
Fadell, Tony, 153
Fairchild Semiconductor, 15
FairSearch (coalition), 148
Federal Bureau of Investigation (FBI), 43
Federal Trade Commission (FTC), 157, 163
Field, Ben, 39, 40
Financial industry
community banks and services, 72, 187, 188, 196
disaggregation, 191–192
regulation, 185–186, 190, 194, 196–197
tech companies challenge traditional banks, 184–192
tech companies could change banking, 193–197
tech companies' entries, 182, 191–192, 194
technology platforms, 189
Fitchard, Kevin, 204–208
Florida, Richard, 60
Food delivery systems, 132–133
Foreign Intelligence Surveillance Act (FISA) Court, 50
Forestry, 81
Fossil fuel-powered energy
industry obstruction, renewables use, 32
sources and usage, 21, 22–24
transitions to renewable, 23–24, 31–32